Evolve

ISBN-13: 9781090786074

Evolve

By
Brian Hunter

Published by

Rainbow Wisdom

Ireland

ABOUT THE AUTHOR

Brian Hunter is an American author and Life Coach based in Los Angeles, California. Brian is the author of *Evolve*, *The Hunter Equation*, *Heal Me*, *Rising To Greatness*, and *The Walk-In*. His books have sold around the world and have been Best Sellers within their genre. Brian was acknowledged as being intuitive as a child, and then later in life was attributed as having psychic abilities, as chronicled in his dramatic memoir *The Walk-In*. Brian has worked with people from all over the world, including celebrities and captains of industry. Brian was an original cast member of the TV series pilot "Missing Peace," in which psychics worked with detectives to solve cold cases. He has also worked as an actor and model in Hollywood, and been featured in various movie and TV productions. Brian's current focus is on his writing and life coaching work, helping clients from all walks of life.

www.brianhunterhelps.com

DEDICATION

I dedicate this book to everyone who has faced loss, pain, suffering, abuse, betrayal, ridicule, and abandonment, yet still hold love within their heart. Also, dedicated to all of those who have the courage to become better than who they presently are.

CONTENTS

CONTENTS

CHAPTER ONE

The Journey

E volve. Evolve into what? Well, I cannot answer that for you exactly. You need to decide YOUR EXACT destination for yourself. If I told you what to do and what to become, you would not be evolving. Okay, good talk. Hope you enjoyed all that wisdom. See you next time.

Wait, don't go! Just kidding! Actually, I want us to take a journey together. An amazing grand journey! Please say you'll come along. Where are we going, might you ask? I am not sure exactly where we will end up, but I know what we are leaving behind. We are leaving behind the old unevolved conditions that leave us stuck and in pain. For many of us, the present conditions on this planet, or in our lives, or within ourselves, no longer serve us. Too many of us live limited lives in a toxic environment poisoned by fear, greed, anger, and misunderstanding. We hurt from losses, betrayals, failures, mistakes, and worst of all, WORST OF ALL, we suffer from an inability to become unstuck from the pain and recycled behaviors enough to find the happiness we seek and deserve.

I also realize that many of you might be perfectly happy with most aspects of your life. That's fine, and congratulations. But this journey is for you also because we can make your life even more awesome if you agree to come along. We are not "just" fixing what is broken. We will also be building new ways of thinking that will make us all more "evolved," powerful, and happy. It'll be awesome, you will see.

However, first we must pack. We cannot take everything with us. You will have to decide what comes with you and what stays behind. I suspect plenty will be left behind. The hurt, the pain, the losses, the disappointments, the old broken ways, broken things, broken promises, broken hearts, and broken dreams. Leave them. Where we are going you won't need them. People who have hurt you, damaged you, victimized you, just forget it. Leave it. All of that is pain that no longer serves you. What no longer serves you needs to be left behind.

Now let me tell you what you should pack to bring with you on this journey. Bring your fondest memories and sensations. Bring those moments of childhood when innocence and hope were very present. Yes, don't forget your innocence. Bring it because you will need it for the journey. Bring your hope as well. Hope is what fuels our journey. Bring your memories and moments that once gave you a zest for life. Fresh air, the smell of freshly cut grass, the sound of a babbling brook, or waves rolling ashore at the lake or ocean. The sunshine on your face while a perfect breeze makes you feel you are in a moment of perfection. A sip of your favorite drink, and bite of your favorite food. BBQ's with good friends and family who made you feel that you belong someplace, however brief or long that feeling lasted. Periods of perfect health when you felt great and had plenty of energy. Bring your best moments with your favorite people. Remember the times of great laughter, but also the moments of great reflection, comfort, and support. Kindness. Bring kindness please. Kindness is popular where we are going.

Bring your music. Please DO bring your favorite music. You can use that where we are going. Please also bring the spirits of all those you have loved that you have lost and are no longer with us. You can bring them also. Bring your pets. Bring anything that gives you joy. We are taking joy with us for sure. We are taking any happiness we currently hold with us, or the happiness we had and want to feel again one day.

Most of all, bring love. Love is the currency used at our destination. It can be used at any time, and it is used often. It is not kept in your wallet or bank account though. It is kept within you. Don't worry, nobody will steal it. It will be safe within you once you learn how to safeguard it.

When I say bring your love, that includes love for yourself and your desire for a better life. All of this is very much a self-care journey. You are going on this journey because you care enough about yourself to give yourself another chance at life, or at least a chance for a better life. Everyone deserves another chance. You deserve another chance. You deserve a chance at a better life. You deserve happiness. Nobody deserves to suffer. Nobody deserves to be left suffering or in pain. Nobody deserves to be abandoned, period. I won't leave you behind. You found this book, and this was my way of finding you. This makes you destined for this journey if you decide to take it.

Again, even if you are content with your present life, surely you have past traumas, wounds, undesirable behaviors, and issues you would like dealt with so you can be more free. Freedom allows you to feel better, live happier, and achieve greater successes. How can anyone not want that? Plus, you already got this book, and I really don't want you to return it, so I beg you to please come along for the ride.

How are we leaving on this journey you ask? Well, I have arranged for the coolest convertible hot rod that is available within your imagination. We will hit the road and head off into the sunset. Yes, that's right, we leave at sunset. The sun is about to go down on the last day of your old life. We will drive off into the cool gorgeous night and never look back. Yeah, please don't look back or you might get car sick. If you get sick in the car, I lose my deposit, so please don't. Oh, and it gets better. I will drive the first night so you can rest. I know you are tired. You have been through a lot. I know you have been through a lot because you would not have wanted to take this journey if you hadn't been ready for a change of some kind, or a life improvement at the very least.

So climb in and off we go! Just enjoy the perfect night air as we drive off under a blanket of stars above. I don't have any GPS guidance to show the way. All I need to do is follow the brightest stars and smell for the ocean air, and I know that is where we want to go. Just relax, let go of the past behind you, and learn to put trust into a better future. Drive onward we go.

Okay, I hope you had a nice rest. We have been driving all night. You don't even know where we are anymore. But one thing is for sure. You are far away from your old life. The scenery is new and fresh. All you can see now is wide open road and majestic mountains that will guide our way during the daytime.

You wish to know where we are going specifically? Well, I am not sure yet. That depends on you. All I know is that we will drive until the land meets the sea. Until then, enjoy the road trip. Let me know if you need to use the restroom. Otherwise, we will keep driving without stopping, because I don't want to risk any distractions so early in our grand adventure. There will be plenty of time for stops later on. Right now, I just want you to enjoy the freedom of the road. Feel the energy of your old life fading behind you. Let it go. Let it all go. What you have now are wide open possibilities in front of you. How does that feel? What would you do with that? It wasn't a rhetorical question. I'll just leave that there for you to contemplate on your own. Just enjoy the wind in your face and the blessing of choice to drive away from the old, and leave what no longer serves you behind. Just drive away until you know the old is behind you, then you know you are getting closer to your destination.

Long drive. Do you smell that? Ocean air. I LOVE the smell of the ocean. It is so refreshing, full of new possibilities, and just brings a sense of freedom with it. The road trip was fun, but it's getting a little cramped in this car, and it's time for us to continue our journey a different way. Let us no longer be limited by the road.

Let's sail away! Let's detach from all the burdens, traumas, and pain that bind us on land, and let's sail away. Climb on board this fabulous sailboat I have arranged for us. No, there is no engine power, but the set of large handsome sails on this beautiful vessel will take us wherever we want to go. She is a fine vessel, and if we learn to work with the wind and nature that surrounds us, she will take us to where we want to go. That's right, you heard correctly. No engines. Engines are so yesterday, and would limit us by the amount of fuel we have, and we would be living on borrowed time until something eventually broke. Things always break, right? So why bother with that? We will trust the wind and the sails that will serve us endlessly with no limits as long as we understand and respect Mother Nature.

Sail away! Find your freedom from the road on the wide-open seas. Now we can venture anywhere, in any direction. We are no longer limited in direction by the roads. Feel the sun on your face and the wind at your back. Hear the sea as it ripples around us ever so lightly. Hear the birds and dolphins that surround us. Be one with the sailboat, the ocean, and the breeze. You are no longer stuck and limited as you were before, but you must focus now. You must focus and be one with the sea, the wind, and all that surrounds you. Don't be distracted by what is no longer important. Don't be distracted by what has hurt you in the past. All that matters now is that you are free to sail the

13

great blue waters to your heart's content.

However, eventually, everything comes to an end. I say it like it's a bad thing, but it's not. One ending means another beginning. We have reached the end of our sailing journey. Now it is time for the next leg of our journey. It is time to fly away.

While on the sea becoming one with the wind, you have grown wings from the freedom of leaving behind what weighted you down and limited you in the past. Now you can fly. If you are afraid at all, you will need to leave your fears behind. You cannot be free and fly away with fear weighting you down. Set your old human fears aside, and for a moment feel life in front of you without fear.

Close your eyes, feel the wind in your face, and extend your wings. Then simply fly away. Feel the freedom you have now as you soar through the air. Feel the wind beneath you that provides you with the life necessary to soar, instead of the heavy resistance of the past keeping you grounded. Instead of slowing you down and keeping you stuck, the wind now lifts you up into the air where you have total freedom. You can see the sun, the bright endless blue skies, the wispy light clouds, and the bright blue ocean beneath you. The wind, sun, perfect air, and total freedom alone, give you a sense of hope and happiness.

What's more, is that now you are flying free in the sky, you can join hands with any loved one no longer on Earth, and you can feel their presence and fly with them. Feel their hand in yours, see their smile as they enjoy the freedom you now share with them, and once again fill your heart with love. Know that they are with you. What was lost is now yours again if you can feel their spirit as you are flying away from all that bound you and limited you in the past. You are never alone, even while flying freely in the sky.

Fly free into a new way of life, with new ways of thinking, behaving, and living. Evolve into a more advanced person capable of far more than ever before. Learn how to release yourself from your limitations, pain, suffering, and weaknesses. Learn how to think and live on a new level that allows you the freedom to fly wherever you want. The journey is only beginning. I can't promise it will always be easy, but I promise it will be amazing. I'm so glad you are here.

CHAPTER TWO

Winds Of Change

W e had the wind in our face on our road trip, the wind at our back on the sailboat, and then the wind under our wings flying free in the sky. The wind has been a constant presence during our journey so far. The funny thing about wind is that it is always out of our control, and it is constantly changing. The thing that has given us so much enjoyment and fuel for our journey is something always changing that we don't control. Most people would consider things we can't control, and that are constantly changing, a bad thing. But in our case, it is our friend. It has enabled us to take our journey. Perhaps we should let the haters keep hating the wind if the lack of control and change annoys them, but we should make friends with it. After all, we are no long embracing the old ways of thinking that no longer serve us. Instead, we are evolving.

Change specifically, is our friend. We are recognizing it as a source to fuel our progress. It's ironic because most people consider change a bad thing that interrupts and blocks their progress, and causes problems. Why is this? Well, humans typically think in terms of very few dimensions. But I am getting ahead of myself, and we will discuss this at length later. Humans tend to view their CURRENT environment and circumstances as their baseline standard of how it is, should be, and will be. They view it more or less as a constant. Then, based off of their current environment and circumstances, they make all of their decisions. Perhaps you can see where I am going with this. This type of thinking is a recipe for disaster. If there is one constant in the Universe, it is that everything always changes eventually.

Thus, humans inevitably, sooner rather than later, end up experiencing change that affects their environment, which then changes their INTENDED outcome. When humans receive an outcome they did not plan for or expect, they typically do not like this, and it can cause all kinds of problems. I am not saying that change is always good and never causes problems. I am only pointing out that basing your expectations on an environment and circumstances that are a constant, is a flawed way of thinking that is guaranteed to lead to problems.

At the very least, everyone should fully assume and factor change into all of their assumptions, planning, and thinking. This basically would be an improvement and the next step up from not factoring in change at all. However, we are going to go further than that. Not only will we factor in change as the biggest constant of the Universe, but we will also view change as a POSITIVE factor in the dynamics of our planning, strategy, and SOLUTIONS.

Another skill we are going to be engaging in on an increasing basis, is the use of logic instead of emotional impulse. Most humans make choices on emotional impulse and this blinds them to clear reasoning of likely outcomes. In this chapter we are going to look at change in a logical way.

Too many people who are struggling with something tend to do the same thing over and over, hoping for a different outcome. They do this because they WANT a certain outcome, and they think if they try the same thing over and over enough times, they might achieve it. This can certainly happen. There are certain things that depend on repetition for success. But mostly, you are more likely to achieve a desired outcome if you can somehow employ the correct strategy, within the correct environment and circumstances, at the correct time.

Thus, if you have been trying to improve your life, or achieve a certain goal, by working hard in the same fashion over and over, for a long period of time, you are not likely to succeed. I am not saying it is not possible for repetition to work. I am just saying it is not as likely to work. Slamming your head against the same brick wall over a long period of time while hoping to achieve your outcome, is only going to give you a headache and maybe brain damage. Can we all agree right here and now to stop doing this? You might be thinking that you are not doing it. However, you might be doing it and not realizing it.

For example, if you are struggling with a difficult relationship that is in a cycle of going smooth for a while, then going off the rails, then a struggle, then smooth, and this cycle over and over, you might ask yourself why you think this cycle will ever change. People often think, "Well, it will be different next time," or "My partner promised to change." But invariably, behaviors, cycles, and life, tend to repeat over and over. Each time we convince ourselves that if we try harder next time, maybe things will turn out differently. Basically, we are doing the same things over and over, hoping that somehow things will turn out differently next time. They almost never do.

The same is true in business. If a person is having trouble making sales, they often think, "Maybe if I work more hours, I will do better," or "Maybe I will get lucky and just achieve more sales because I am thinking more positive." But if the person is still using the same sales strategies, on the same customer base, with the same product, it is likely nothing will change for them. WANTING a better result will not give you a better result. HOPING things will somehow work out better next time will likely not give you a better result. Hope is for inspiration in surviving life, not for ignoring the need for real change.

Whether people realize it or not, they are likely repeating the same strategies and behaviors while hoping and wanting a different result. We have to evolve from that into a higher dimension of thinking that is more effective. This means that when something is not working well for us, we need to recognize that we must initiate CHANGE in a substantial way. I do not mean changing from one positive thought to another positive thought. I don't mean changing to a different lucky tie at work. What I mean is that you must realize your current strategy, behavior, and thinking, is not working. Take a moment on that. Breathe. There needs to be that moment when you pause, and REALIZE it is NOT working. So stop. CHANGE. Not only change, but make the change substantial and perhaps even drastic. You cannot change your life and get a different result if you don't ACTUALLY change. Maybe read that one again. It sounds simple and not much of an evolution, but it's actually huge because most people do not do it. Therefore, that makes it substantial and important. You must recognize change as vitally important and valuable. Change will be the key to your success and happiness in the future. By changing your strategies, behavior, and environment, you can change your life, outcome, and results.

Why wouldn't you want to do that? Well, maybe you are afraid of change. We will talk much more about fear a bit later, but if I say it once, I will say it many times, that you will need to set fear aside in order to evolve. You cannot be afraid of change. You must embrace change. You must look for change. You must seek ways in which to implement change. Change will be something you proactively pursue,

19

rather than hide from or remain in denial.

There will be some heavy lifting in this book if you are using our journey as a method of personal transformation. You must be willing to accept, embrace, and make change. If you don't do this, then our journey is just a temporary reprieve. You are flying high with the eagles at the moment. You are flying free and have all possibilities open to you. However, you can't stay in the air forever. Even the greatest and strongest eagles must land from time to time. They must land back on Earth where reality reigns.

We drove off into the sunset in that fancy fun convertible. We drove away from the old life of pain and struggle where things do not change much, or enough. If we just ended our story here, you would find that you were only running away from your problems rather than solving them. Your old life and all that came with it would eventually catch up with you. We are not on this journey to run and hide temporarily. We are on this journey to evolve so that life can be different and better.

The first step in ensuring a successful journey is that you decide to engage with change. Don't go back. We are having fun so far, aren't we? So, let's keep going. If you agree, then you need to consider what changes you might need to make. I will give you a hint in order to get you started. Think of all the things that give you pain. Those are likely the things that need to change. Write them down if you want. Remember, we are engaging with logic more often now, and part of logic is making lists. Lists allow us to see things clearly so they can't be forgotten or avoided as easily.

Think of all the things you left behind, and wish to stay behind, and never wish for them to catch up with you again in the future. They are things that you either didn't need anymore, or were things that caused you pain. Write them down. They may be specific circumstances, events, places, things, people, problems, feelings, behaviors, habits, cycles, or toxicity. It can be anything that has hurt you, makes you suffer, struggle, remain in pain, or remain stuck. Those are all the things you need to identify and mark for change.

I obviously cannot go into great detail on how to change each and every issue you have written down. However, my book *Heal Me* goes into detailed discussions about healing from a large variety of life traumas and difficulties. For our purposes in this book, we need to remain focused on the general concept of change so that we can directly cause solutions for our various items of pain we have noted.

With that said, I will discuss a useful concept of affecting change. In our examples, we have left items behind that no longer serve us. They are items that need to be changed so that they remain behind and don't catch up with us again in the future. We will call that "the darkness." Then, there are the items we packed and brought with us on our journey. Those were things you wanted to keep with you. Those things still serve you, they mean something to you, provide you with comfort and happiness, or they inspire you and give you joy. We will call those items "the light."

The idea now is to provide as much separation as possible between the darkness and the light. You can do that by disconnecting from the darkness as much as possible, and embracing the light as closely as possible. It is easier to leave something when you have something else to go toward. Thus, you want to use your items of light as a distraction that will occupy your attention. You have things you enjoy such as pets, people, hobbies, activities, memories, music, and other items. You will want to INCREASE your engagement with those items. Increasing your closeness with these items will help you disconnect from the old items of darkness. Go toward the light. Leave the darkness. So, if you also want to make a list of your "items of light," also, feel free.

People going through times of change usually find comfort in clinging to things that are not changing. Start listening to your old music you had forgotten about that will give you joyous

21

memories. Spend more time with your pets than before. Go visit an old friend that you have not had time for in a while. Visit old places that used to give you wonderful feelings and good times. Increase your involvement in hobbies, exercise, or activities that you have enjoyed in the past and present. You get the idea.

You need to examine the items in the darkness. Decide what needs to be changed, as in taken apart and put back together in a different way. Also examine what needs to be changed, as in no longer having it in your life. While you are doing this to the items of the darkness, you are more fully involving yourself with the items of light. Using this method will help you in your process of change.

Change is your passport to freedom. If you enjoy soaring like an eagle in the sky, free from all the limitations back on the ground, and all possibilities in the sky surrounding you in all directions, then never forget that none of this is possible without CHANGE. For those of you resistant to change for one reason or another, you will have to constantly remind yourself that change is the key to endless possibilities and freedom. If you remember this, you will begin to recognize change as something to run toward and embrace.

Change is your friend, and it loves you. It wants to free you from your current pain and struggles. Change is the wind. It is constant and unpredictable. It can blow in your face and seem difficult, or it can blow in your face and seem refreshing. Let change fill your sails with power, and provide lift under your wings so you can fly free in the sky like an eagle. Fly in the winds of change so you can evolve.

CHAPTER THREE

Human Frailties

It's tough being a human. While humans are amazing with their wide range of emotions, they are also fraught with almost endless frailties that can doom them to a life of struggle, failure, and lack of progress. It's almost as if our creator said, "I grant you the widest range of emotions and sensations possible, and let's see if they destroy you or not."

In the last chapter we discussed the need to change. We decided the items to be targeted for change are all the items you left behind, in the hope they would stay behind. The only way for issues to stay behind is to address them and resolve them. I also mentioned we could not cover all of the issues you likely want to change, but I want to at least address some of the issues at this time so you can at least see the thought process of identifying, confronting, and changing some of these issues.

I cannot possibly go into too much detail on each issue, with this being only one chapter. However, I do address many of these issues in greater detail, as well as solutions for dealing with them, in my books *Heal Me* and *Rising To Greatness*, if you have not looked at those already. We are on a very long important journey presently, and while I must be brief, it is still critically important we learn how to deal with human frailties. With that said, there is plenty of heavy lifting to do in this chapter with all the issues I want to briefly cover, and I ask for your patience as we go through them. I promise things get more interesting and fun as we move beyond some of the fundamental issues.

The best part of being human is also the worst part of being human. Of the many species of creatures in the Universe, I am willing to bet that humans are among those with the highest level of emotional sensitivity. Humans are so emotional that it can literally prevent them from functioning. If you examine all of your worst issues, most of them involve emotions. Very often we experience things in life that traumatize us emotionally and cause us to suffer for long periods of time. While we cannot take emotions out of our humanity, nor would we want to, what we CAN DO is endeavor to cope with these emotionally based issues more productively.

Remember, what we are doing here is trying to evolve. Evolving requires us to CHANGE. Therefore, let us examine some common issues and see if we can identify even the smallest ways that we can change, in order to improve how we function and live our lives.

DEPRESSION

The biggest issue I see when dealing with clients and observing life is Depression with a big D. Depression is often the result of an emotional trauma or traumatic/negative life circumstance. Yes, it can be chemical also, but even then, some event or condition usually triggers it. When a traumatic event or circumstance surrounds you, that causes the "Depression Monster" to move inside your head. He lives there rent free. The monster always knows what to whisper in your ear that will trigger you into despair, which keeps you under the control of the monster. It is a cycle that is hard to break. Even if you start to feel better, the monster usually comes up with just the right thing to whisper in your ear to bring you back down again. The monster controls you because it knows your deepest thoughts and fears, and it knows all your trigger points. The monster knows what to whisper, and when, so that it can have the maximum effect of keeping you in despair. What is the monster's motivation? It wants to keep you in misery at the least, and it wants to kill you at most.

What is the solution to this? Aside from various coping mechanisms I cover in my other books I mentioned previously, the silver bullet involves CHANGE. Ultimately, you must make a number of changes. You must change how you deal with the monster in your head, and you must make some environmental changes.

You must change by no longer listening to the monster. Depression keeps you captive because you keep listening to the whispers in your head. Those whispers keep you under the control of depression because the whispers are designed to keep HOPE very far away from you, and the whispers are designed to keep you too weakened in order to fight off the depression. The whispers are designed to keep you in despair. The change you must make is to STOP LISTENING. What I mean by this is that when you hear those whispers that always trigger you and keep you in depression, you need to disregard them and ignore them.

You need to realize that all the whispers are LIES. They are lies designed only to trigger you and control you. Stop listening and believing the lies! When you hear those whispers, say to yourself, "No, I am not listening anymore." You need to realize the monster is trying to attack you, and you should engage in your coping mechanisms, which may include going for a walk, listening to music, or whatever works for you. The key is that you no longer agree to listen to those whispers. That is the mental change you must make.

You likely also need to make environmental changes, meaning changes to what surrounds you, or your circumstances. If another person is causing the depression, you will have to CHANGE by disconnecting from them to some degree or another. If a lifestyle habit is causing the depression, you need to change by stopping or altering it. Sometimes you may even need to move, or change jobs, or get involved in new activities. Exercise is one of the best treatments for depression that I know. The point is that you need to most definitely make changes within your environment and circumstances.

If you refuse to engage in change, you will find it difficult to defeat depression. Please never forget what you left behind in the darkness on this journey, and how wonderful it felt soaring in the air free as a bird with all the possibilities of life open to you. Make the right choice out of love for yourself. Make the necessary changes. I believe in you and know you can do it. I wouldn't suggest it otherwise.

LOSS/GRIEF

Humans do not handle loss and grief very well. We tend to get VERY ATTACHED to certain people (and pets). When we lose them, it can literally cause our entire world to crumble down around us so that we feel nothing is left, and our lives are gone and over. This can leave us in a state of mind that causes us to stop living life, and have to endure immense pain that paralyzes us and prevents us from functioning.

Can I fix a loss? Can I bring back who you lost so that everything is okay? No, I cannot. Making it so that nobody ever dies is not going to be one of the solutions we have to work with. Life is beautiful because it's precious. It is precious because it's finite. The most precious things in life are those that are fleeting. Moments, smells, tastes, feelings, they are all the best sensations of life, and they are all fleeting. Fortunately, human life lasts for a longer period of time, but it still comes to an end eventually. We should treasure it, and everybody in it.

If I cannot stop people from dying and I cannot revive those who have already died, how do I propose to fix this particular problem? My suggestion is to change how we think about death, and deal with death. First, you need to appreciate what I said earlier about how life is precious because it does not last forever. Be grateful for that. We know that we all must eventually leave this life journey to start another journey. We must respect and appreciate that our loved one received this privilege. We all have different religious and spiritual beliefs, but most of us can agree that death is a transition to some other state of being or place, however active or inactive that may be, according to your own beliefs.

I want to make it clear that I respect beliefs that are different from mine. Please do not feel that I am trying in any way to convince you of my own beliefs, or change your beliefs. One thing I will not be seeking to CHANGE, are your core religious and spiritual beliefs.

With that said, I will give my thoughts and suggestions on dealing with death from my perspective, as the author. My belief is that humans have a soul, which consists of eternal energy. I go into my theories in great detail within my book *The Hunter Equation*. But briefly, I believe we have a soul of energy that exists eternally. When the body dies, that "soul energy" returns "home" "to God" "to the Universe." But that "consciousness" still exists within that energy. I am not making all of this up just because I want it to be true. I actually believe in the concept of "Conservation of Energy." Like matter, energy does not just vanish into nothingness. Energy simply changes forms and locations. It goes somewhere. So, if the soul consists of energy, that energy must go somewhere. It still exists. Thus, that consciousness within that energy will still exist as well.

27

The above theory and principle is what "psychic mediumship" is based upon. This is when psychic mediums claim to "connect" and "communicate" with deceased loved ones. Obviously, some of these claims may be false, but I believe plenty of them are legitimate and real. You can have your own opinion and beliefs about this. But if the energy and consciousness of a person still exists out there somewhere, it makes sense that a person who is able to connect to such "frequencies" would be able to sense or even communicate with this consciousness.

My point with this discussion is that I believe we need to CHANGE how we think of death and deal with death. Instead of considering the person, all they were, and their "essence", as being gone, we need to believe that somehow, in some way, they still exist. We just need to learn how to tune into this belief and incorporate it into our minds and hearts. We need to keep our loved one with us. We need to bring them with us on our journey. They are not totally gone. Their energy, their consciousness, their essence, it still exists out there. Let's tune into that and keep it. Similar to how a psychic or psychic medium can tune into this, so can you. I am going to teach you how to do this in a later chapter. Yes, I just said that.

So please keep faith and know that we can make it better. While I cannot bring back your loved one, we can work together to help you build a connection with them so that you still feel them with you. Once you feel they are with you on your own continued journey, you can take some comfort in that, and know all is not lost. They can remain with you. Life is full of blessings if we know where to look, and are willing to change how we think and live. This is one of those opportunities.

SADNESS

Sadness is a valid human emotion that is part of our normal healthy response to being a human. I would not seek to eliminate sadness. We need to be allowed to feel sad sometimes about things that are, well, sad. What I seek to do is change how we process and deal with sadness.

When something happens to us that make us unhappy, we sometimes become sad. Maybe something did not work out how we were hoping. Maybe someone did something mean to us. Or perhaps there are circumstances in our life that make us sad. For whatever reason, we feel sadness.

It is actually healthy to feel sadness when it's appropriate. People who feel nothing are machines and likely suppressing their human emotions until they develop a more serious issue later on. Sadness needs to be experienced, felt, and processed. It should come, you feel it, and then it should fade and leave. Sadness only becomes a serious problem when it does not go away. Sadness that does not go away can make us depressed and miserable. We can't have that. I trust that you intended to leave any lasting sadness back in the darkness which we left behind. However, if we don't want it to catch up and find us, we still must deal with it, like all the other issues we left behind.

To keep sadness back where it belongs, we must change how we think of sadness. While we allow sadness to come, and we allow ourselves to feel it and experience it, we can no longer allow it to stay. We must make changes to how we think of sadness so that it LEAVES, as it is supposed to.

My belief and suggestion is to turn the sadness into something else other than just sadness. You will have to decide the exact thoughts and pathways that work best for you, but I will give you a couple examples of how to deal with it.

If I am feeling sadness because of how someone treated me, I turn my sadness into empathy and love. I feel my sadness, I decide that it's horrible and I do not wish it upon anyone, including myself. I realize what caused the sadness might have been unfair treatment or lack of compassion toward me. It might have been a lack of understanding, love, or empathy. The correct response to this would be to increase the amount of love and empathy you show others and yourself. I take my sadness and transfer it into love and empathy by engaging in self-care for myself, knowing I deserved better. I transfer it into love and empathy by proactively showing more kindness, love, and empathy toward someone who might really need it because they are also feeling sadness.

This technique can be called "Becoming The Solution." You take a problem that someone dumped onto you, and you become the solution by dumping the OPPOSITE onto someone else. Isaac Newton stated that "for every action there is an equal and opposite reaction." Instead of being miserable, bitter, and mean from how you were treated, you can show compassion and caring toward someone else instead. What this does is it changes the energetic equation of the event and emotion. Instead of allowing the negative emotion to continue, by continuing it unto others, you have stopped it by no longer continuing it, AND by actually starting a chain of something more positive toward others.

The act of doing this makes you feel better because in a sense you have created your own sense of justice by stopping the continuance of the negativity. You have treated others how you wish you had been treated. You have taken the high road. You have contributed to the world by stopping a negative and starting a positive. You should feel good about this. This should give you some relief from your sadness knowing how you were able to change the entire energy of the emotional situation. You will notice that I never said you had to respond this way toward the same person who did you wrong. We are not interested in rewarding bad behavior. My suggestion was to respond to SOMEONE ELSE with kindness who needs it and might value it.

Another example might be that I am sad because something did not work out the way I had hoped. I am going to transfer this sadness into motivation. I am going to recognize that sometimes things require many tries, or trying in different ways, or using different strategies, with different people. Sometimes the timing is just off, and trying again at a different time will work better.

Instead of moping around in defeat, I will take my sadness and use it as fuel to check for any mistakes I made, or improvements I can make for next time. I will see what could be CHANGED within the situation to make it successful or work out better next time. This sadness has now become a reason to be motivated and hopeful for a better outcome next time.

The bottom-line regarding sadness is that you cannot allow it to remain. You cannot allow yourself to remain in it for long periods of time. You must take some kind of action. You must change. You must make changes. You cannot simply do nothing. Take that sadness and transfer it into something more useful. Sadness is such a common and huge issue that we will continue discussion it in more depth within the next chapter.

ANGER

Like sadness, anger is a normal human emotion that should come, be felt, and leave. The difference between sadness and anger is that anger should be released immediately, while sadness can linger long enough for us to contemplate what happened to us and why. Anger should be released immediately because it can be a more volatile and destructive emotion. Nothing good ever happens when someone is angry. If a person is angry, they will make bad decisions for certain, and they may even take some destructive actions they will regret.

If you are a person who experiences anger often, you must change. You need to change so that you are releasing your anger immediately after experiencing it. The method for doing this will be to always remind yourself that anger can only hurt you. Only bad things can happen under the influence of anger. Train your mind to immediately remind yourself that anger can only hurt you, and never help you. That's step one. Step two would be to engage your coping mechanisms that will help to reduce your anger to dust and smoke, and let it blow away. Again, this might mean going for a walk, exercising, or whatever you need to do. But you must engage in a behavior that allows you to shed your anger as quickly as it arrived. Do not just allow it to fester, build, and exist within you. CHANGE by taking steps and creating coping mechanisms to immediately release anger in a harmless way. Your life will improve, I assure you.

SELF-ESTEEM ISSUES

Many humans experience self-esteem issues, meaning a low self-esteem. Yes, some can experience a self-esteem that is too high that results in arrogance. But we will focus on low self-esteem because it affects almost everyone at some point in their lives in a very longer-term negative way.

Low self-esteem usually happens when someone in your life made you feel less than what you are. It could have been a parent, romantic partner, a boss, or people in your social circle. It can also be the general public. Humans have very delicate psyches and are very vulnerable to mental conditioning and brainwashing. Negative mental conditioning is called abuse.

All it takes is a significant person in your life to abuse you in some way, mentally or physically. A process of abuse or negative mental conditioning will most certainly lower a person's self-esteem. The reason is because you start to believe what they are saying to you. You start to believe that maybe you are being mistreated because you don't deserve good treatment. And if you don't deserve good treatment, that must mean you are less of a person. Thus, you now have a low self-esteem. Obviously, this is a very brief simplification of the dynamics involved.

The solution is to change how you are being affected by the abuse and negative mental conditioning. Very similar to the depression monster, you must realize the input is invalid and lies. You must decide to no longer believe the negative mental conditioning. Just as important, is that you need to somehow disconnect and leave that environment so that you are no longer subjected to it. It is a lot easier to stop listening to the negative mental conditioning if you are no longer near the source of it.

After you have disconnected and stopped believing in it, you can slowly repair your self-esteem by engaging in positive mental conditioning that will help rebuild your self-esteem.

NEED FOR OUTSIDE VALIDATION

All humans are kind of born seeking outside validation. As young children we seek approval from our parents. This is when it starts. Then it just grows from there. We need others to tell us we are worthy and good. We seek it from teachers, bosses, friends, and pretty much everyone. We have to have someone telling us we are worthy. This is outside validation.

The problem is that we can become a slave to this. A couple different problems can result. We can get to the point that a person can totally control our actions by dangling positive validation in front of us if we do certain things, even if we know those things are wrong. An example would be when kids join a gang because the need for validation is more important than the fact they will be asked to do things they know are wrong.

An additional problem is that if we don't receive the outside validation, we naturally assume that we are not worthy of validation. This can damage our self-esteem. Thus, we are desperate for this outside validation so that we can feel worthy as a person. It's all the same thing really. Outside validation is a crutch that we come to depend on in order to feel valued as a person. It has to go.

The change I am seeking here, is to throw out the need for outside validation into the garbage. It is useless except to stroke the ego. Its downside far exceeds any upside for your ego. Stop depending on others to validate your value. If you depend on others for validation, they control you because they can withhold it or give it, at their whim. Do not allow yourself to be controlled in that manner. You cannot truly be free, evolve, and thrive, until you move away from needing outside validation.

ADDICTION

I hesitated about including addiction into this chapter because it is such a large issue and topic, which belongs in an entirely separate book or multiple books. However, how can I avoid an issue that affects almost everyone in some way? Whether it be a direct issue for you, or an indirect issue because it affects someone you know, it touches everyone in some way. Addiction can be something as serious as heavy drug use, something as common as alcoholism and smoking, or more minor things like food addiction (which isn't that minor health-wise).

Humans are very susceptible to falling into some kind of addiction. Why is this? Well, it goes back to the fact that humans are very vulnerable to heavy emotions that affect them mentally in such a way that they can barely cope.

The addiction itself is usually a result of needing a way to escape or avoid the pain of their emotions. Some fall into addiction purposely because they so desperately need some relief from their mental or physical pain. Others fall into it by accident, by experimenting casually, and one thing leads to another. The bottom line is that addiction is usually a result of needing relief from pain of some kind.

Again, I cannot give a solution to this problem in a few paragraphs. But I will say this. Until you deal with your addictions, they will keep you stuck to some degree. It is hard to fully evolve while under the control of some foreign substance or habit.

In general, and I do mean VERY GENERALLY, addiction treatment involves three major steps. First, you must break the chemical dependance. You can go cold turkey, or you can seek professional help. You need to detox and break the actual physical dependance. Don't be afraid to ask your doctor or a professional about helping you with this. There is not much you can do mentally about chemical dependence, so there is no shame in getting help with this.

Secondly, you need to identify the core issues that caused you to have the addiction in the first place. This is the psychological or mental part of the treatment. Counseling is very important so that you can realize WHY you need what you need and do what you do. Once you identify the core issue, you can work to resolve that issue so that you no longer NEED the addiction.

Finally, you need to also make lifestyle and environmental changes so that you are less likely to re-engage with the addiction. You need to remove all the triggers from your life, whatever they may be.

Addiction is dealt with by deciding to make the change. It always seems to come down to embracing and engaging with change, doesn't it?

REPEATING PATTERNS

Humans have a very bad habit of repeating bad patterns and behaviors over and over. We only need to examine a person's romantic relationships to see this in play. Of course, not everyone is afflicted by this issue, so I am not pointing fingers at you or anyone else. But we have all seen people who seem to repeat the same bad relationships, by attracting, or being attracted to, the same bad actors that result in the same bad relationships. We see repeating patterns with addiction as well obviously. You can find repeating patterns within most human behaviors and life situations.

The famous saying goes, "Doing the same thing over and over again while expecting a different result, is the definition of insanity." There is plenty of truth to that statement. It is for this reason that we must fully see and acknowledge any negative and destructive repeating patterns we might be engaging in, and break the cycle.

The most effective way to break a cycle of a bad pattern is to clearly see you are doing it. Then when you find yourself slipping back into the familiar pattern, purposely do something different, even if it feels unnatural and wrong. At a certain point, taking a different wrong action is better than continuing to repeat the same old destructive pattern.

LACK OF DISCIPLINE

Most of us from time to time suffer from a lack of discipline. Discipline is quite difficult for humans, as it runs against our natural tendencies. Humans by nature only want to do what they want to do, when they want to do it. Humans do not like to do things they don't enjoy, or when they don't want to do them. Discipline is tough, but discipline is necessary for a successful and productive life.

In my book *Heal Me*, I outline in detail a great approach to bring discipline into your life called "Structured Task-driven Lifestyle." With this approach, you break down your day into segments, and insert the tasks that need to be done into the segments of your day. Being disciplined has everything to do with what structure and coping mechanisms you put into place to trick or force yourself to get things done.

LACK OF MOTIVATION

A lack of motivation is not to be confused with a lack of discipline. While a lack of discipline is a function of structure and coping mechanisms, a lack of motivation is more a function of a lack of realistic inspiring goals.

Motivation is all about incentive. If there is no incentive, there is no motivation. Thus, the cure to having a lack of motivation is to put in place adequate incentives. An incentive can be a larger overall goal or reward you want to achieve, or it can be some kind of smaller reward for completing a task. Without motivation you will struggle, so if you suffer from this, you ought to look seriously at your life goals, and how you are rewarding yourself for completing important and unimportant tasks along the way.

THINKING WITH EMOTIONS INSTEAD OF LOGIC

Sadly, this failing is simply a symptom of being human. Humans tend to get emotional and make their decisions while emotional, and by using emotion. I hope I am not the only person to see how flawed this approach is.

Decisions should only be made when a person is calm and thinking clearly. Decisions should be made after clearly examining and considering all evidence, potential solutions, and choices. Decisions should be made using logic and reason. We will be discussing this more later.

I cannot cover every human frailty in this chapter, or even in this book. But I urge you to take inventory of what you perceive to be your own frailties or weaknesses. We can chalk up some frailties to being human, but most of them would need to be addressed and resolved in order for you to evolve up to your full potential. I do not judge you for your frailties, just like I would not want to be judged for mine. We are on an amazing journey to change our lives and evolve. We can do this together!

CHAPTER FOUR

Putting Sadness In Its Place

We already discussed sadness in the previous chapter, but it is such a common and important affliction that we need to examine it in more detail so that we can truly understand it, and make sure it stays in its place rather than blocking our ability to evolve and be happy.

As we previously mentioned, sadness is a normal healthy human emotion that everyone experiences. We cannot and would not want to totally eliminate sadness from our pallet of emotional experiences. However, many people experience levels of sadness so profound that it becomes debilitating, and turns to depression. I think it's fair to have a deeper discussion about sadness, as it is necessary to more fully understand it and contain it, in order to evolve into a healthier, happier, more productive person.

For the purposes of this particular discussion of sadness in this chapter, I want to divide sadness into two different types. First, we have "typical sadness," which is a normal consequence of something not going our way in life. Perhaps a person might have said something insensitive or mean to us that made us feel sad. Or perhaps a friend cancelled a planned outing that we were really looking forward to doing. Or, maybe the ice cream shop was out of your favorite flavor. These are examples of "typical sadness" because it is a sadness that is a healthy and normal response to something we feel as negative toward us. This is the type of sadness I alluded to earlier as a healthy sadness humans cannot escape, nor should we escape. This type of sadness comes and goes. We feel it, experience it, process it, and it fades away as we move beyond it.

I don't expect humans to evolve beyond a normal level of sadness that humans experience from time to time. I am far more concerned about what we will call a "deep sadness" that sits within us for long periods of time, and in some cases, never leaves. "Deep sadness" tends to result from major life events, or events that seem major to us, even if they are not as major to outside third parties. Some examples that result in a deep sadness include loss of loved ones (including pets), the ending of significant relationships, terminations of major career positions, family disputes, difficult life circumstances, major struggles, and basically anything that leaves us feeling that we were failed in some way (including by ourselves), or left abandoned and alone.

Notice the last word of the previous sentence, "alone." Deep sadness leaves us feeling alone. Remember, the cause is usually some sort of loss, betrayal, or major change that shakes our foundation. These things more often than not all leave us feeling alone in some way. We were counting on someone, or some thing, and now they, or it, is gone, leaving us ALONE.

40

The feeling of this sadness combined with aloneness is so profound that it is difficult to describe in words. Unfortunately, most everyone has experienced this, thus I don't have to worry about many people not understanding it. The deep sadness can leave us broken and unable to function at productive levels. A deep sadness makes experiencing happiness almost impossible, except for brief moments when we forget about our real lives. But reality is never far away and always comes back in short order, leaving us back in our deep sadness, feeling alone.

I want to acknowledge everyone feeling this presently. I see you. I hear you. I feel you. I know the pain you feel, as I have felt it myself more than I care to describe. I know some of you hide it well, while others of you cannot even leave your home because you can't hide it. You may have been suffering from a major trauma recently, or you may have been suffering from this deep sadness for many years. It is a feeling that wraps around our heart and soul and never leaves. The fundamental problem is that it steals most of the joy and happiness we could be experiencing in life. It is stealing life itself.

I cannot wave a magic wand and fix this for you. I cannot take back the event that may have initiated this sadness. I cannot change life events that have already happened. But I want to help you see some light, and a pathway to a better life. We started this journey stuck in an old life. We hit the road, we sailed the wide-open seas, and then we soared like an Eagle. How wonderful the feeling of flying free like an eagle. All the burdens of Earth, and the blankets of sadness attached to them, were gone, if only briefly while in flight. I want you to remember how that feels. I want you to remember the lighter feeling in your heart and soul of flying in the sky, surrounded by nothing but beauty, freedom, possibilities, and hope. Listen to me. You can live again. Your heart can open again so that joy and happiness can once again find its way inside.

In order to fix and evolve from serious issues, we must be willing and wanting to CHANGE. We also must not be afraid to face our demons. We must not be afraid to FEEL. We must not be afraid to cry. We must not be afraid to allow ourselves to move forward so we can live again. Let us start by facing the demon of sadness a bit more closely.

Here is all you need to know. Are you ready? The root of deep sadness is actually a lack of love. Allow me to explain. Whatever caused your deep sadness can be traced back to a loss of love. If you lost a dear loved one, you are missing that love and support you had with them within that connection. It does not matter if you did most of the loving or most of the being loved. Either way, that connection was lost. When we feel a connection to someone, we feel loved. We don't need to see them every day. We don't need to hear or say "I love you" very often or at all. The magic is in the fact that we know they are there for us. This connection is a security blanket for our soul. Our soul needs to know someone loves us and is available for the times that we need reminding of this. We need this person to also know that there is a target for us to aim our own love toward. We feel love when we give love and when we receive love, or know that there is love available for us to receive if and when we need it.

Our soul, heart, and mind require this love. When we lose this connection, it is devastating to our soul, heart, and psyche. Without this connection, we feel we have lost our security blanket, source, and outlet, for love. Without love we feel very alone. Without love, we feel deeply sad.

I used the example of when we have lost a loved one, but the concept works for other situations or circumstances you care to use. When we are betrayed or abandoned by friends, family, or romantic partners, we also lose that close connection where we felt we had a source and outlet for love and support. When we lose something important to us, like a job, career position, or home, we have also lost a source of love in our life. When we lose respect or confidence within

42

ourselves, we lose love we had within us for ourselves and our lives. Any kind of loss that results in the destruction of a connection that was a source of love, joy, or support, can result in a deep sadness. I can't change the loss which happened to you that resulted in your sadness. But maybe we can realize ways to evolve from it, so that we can once again fly free like an eagle and live again.

We have established that the root of our deep sadness is a loss, or lack of, love and support that we felt we previously had. You cannot replace the person or exact thing that you previously associated your connection with, but you can try to seek out new sources for a new love you can feel deeply about, and rely on to fuel your inspiration to live and feel joy and happiness.

This does not happen overnight. It takes some commitment and mental conditioning, but you can do it, I know you can. You can choose your own motivation. It may be to honor a lost loved one, who would certainly want you to soar like an eagle and be happy in life. Or, your motivation can be out of your own hope and love deep within YOURSELF, and that you want to give yourself another chance at living life to the fullest again. Whatever your motivation, the effort is worth it.

Whenever I am working with someone who is suffering from great sadness or depression, we often have to start with baby steps and work our way up. Don't be afraid to start small. Starting small means invoking coping mechanisms that allow you to take one more step tomorrow that you did not take today.

Engaging in outside activities, exercise, or in new or old hobbies, can be a great source of coping mechanisms. You have to get back out into the sunlight again, both literally and figuratively. This is the first step.

The next step will be to explore existing or new connections in your life that could serve as new potential sources of love and support in your life, both giving and receiving. There is no way you can replace exactly what you had. We are not trying to replace people we lost, or unique situations we had. We are trying to find new and different connections that can give us what we are seeking. These connections are often hiding in places you never suspected. The connections might involve people you have left on the sidelines for years, or might involve new people you never considered or met before.

You might find new inspirational feelings of love from old or new activities that you renew, such as hiking, travel, music, or other creative ideas you can come up with. Just like lost connections of love can be "things" such as careers or homes, these important connections can also come from new things or activities. People often go back to nature and find their connections, or find themselves that way. It is time for you to explore all possibilities.

But now let me suggest a more evolved approach to the problem. The original problem was caused by us losing a connection to some outside source that we did not control. Since we did not control it, that connection was always vulnerable to leaving us at any time without us being able to do much about it. We were vulnerable all along, and likely, eventually, we were definitely going to lose one or more of our connections, since they were outside of our control.

Thus, the evolved solution is to build a connection with a source that is more stable, immovable, and more within your control. This does not mean you should abandon or not build any traditional connections outside your control. I am not suggesting that at all. In fact, I am suggesting you build as many connections as possible, all in different ways and areas. But with that said, I AM suggesting that you ALSO start building connections that are within your control.

What are some examples of this you ask? The obvious examples in my mind at the moment might include activities, sports, hobbies, and communities that give you incredible passion and joy, as well as a deeper connection to your inner self, and also a deep connection to a chosen spiritual connection or religious faith. Those are things that are within your control and are not likely to just vanish without warning. Obviously, if you choose rock climbing as your passion, and you become seriously injured, that could be an issue. But overall, the suggestions above are very reliable ideas.

Remember, the thing that keeps sadness at bay, is a knowing that you love, and are loved. You need that connection with some source of love. Each person will interpret that differently, and can engage in different ways that is right for you at your level of evolution.

When I suggested that a person develop a stronger connection with their inner self for a source of love, I am sure many people may have rolled their eyes and have no idea how that can work, or what that even means. That is fine. If something does not resonate with you, leave it aside. But others will understand what I am talking about, and it might be a valid suggestion for some. I will admit and agree that having a connection with "self," which is so deep and meaningful it gives you a sense of love and belief within yourself, that the concept is difficult for many. Even so, it is evolved and belongs in this chapter.

More common I suspect, will be the idea of building a strong loving connection with your spiritual or religious beliefs. When you truly believe and FEEL that "Source," "God," "the Universe," "Earth," or whatever your chosen sources are, that it loves you deeply, then you will always feel that love and support within your soul. When you start to truly feel this love within you, your sadness will begin fade.

It is not for me to decide where you find this connection, or to judge what you choose. I am only trying to show you some light and a pathway forward. You get to decide if you want to change your current state of mind and walk the path or not. You can do it when you decide you are ready.

The important thing is that you realize that love is what you lost, and love is the solution. Humans need love. If you find yourself alone and having lost your connection to love, I hope you consider reaching out, up, and within, toward hope and a better life. We love you and

45

do not want to see you suffer. We want to see you living with joy and happiness as an evolved loving person.

CHAPTER FIVE

Controlling Fear

Missing from the "Human Frailties" chapter was a discussion of fear. This is because fear is such a major issue preventing humans from evolving that it needs a chapter of its own. Along with the unwillingness to change, fear is an equally large obstacle to progress.

Whether a person carries fear or not is what separates an ordinary person from a powerful person. A powerful person has no fear. A person mired in fear is at the mercy of the fear itself, along with anyone who uses it against them for control.

There is nothing to fear but fear itself. This is because fear itself is terrifying. Fear will steal your freedom. Fear will cause you to be under the control of whomever weaponizes it against you. Fear will paralyze you into not making decisions or taking actions. If Evil could choose only one weapon to use against you, it would choose fear.

When I said fear is terrifying, what I meant is that it's terrifying what living in fear can do to your life. Whatever it is that you could be afraid of is not nearly as scary as the consequences the fear itself will have on your life.

Most people are probably expecting me to talk about the clichéd reasons of why fear is bad. Fear keeps you from taking the leap. Fear prevents you from taking chances and taking actions that you should possibly take. If you are afraid to do what you feel and know to be right, then you are stuck and never progress. This is the kind of fear most everyone reads about.

I want to focus more on a different kind of fear, a much more dubious, evil, and dangerous fear. I want to focus on the real reason you need to become fearless. Even more destructive than fear holding you back from taking actions, is the idea that fear can be weaponized and used against you. To me, this is much more terrifying than simply being afraid to take a chance on something.

If you have been used, abused, and victimized at some point in your life, it has likely been because fear was used against you as a weapon. Whether it be a romantic partner, employer, family member, or someone else who victimized you, they most surely used fear as one of their weapons, if not the primary weapon.

To understand this, one needs to understand the cycle of abuse. Usually, the victim is somewhat vulnerable from some past traumatic event or abuse. An abuser can smell out victims like a lion smells potential prey. An abuser only needs a whiff of slight weakness to get a foot in the door. The abuser will first identify what you are afraid of. It might be multiple things you are afraid of. They may determine you are afraid of a traumatic event or circumstance happening to you again. They might see you are afraid of being alone or ending up alone. They might see you are afraid you will fail, or that you cannot succeed without help. They will sniff out all of your fears and list them as if they are taking an inventory.

Once they have a list of all your fears, they will test those fears by triggering you to see your fear reactions. So yes, they will trigger you and traumatize you on purpose. But then they will very quickly move onto the next phase. They will then offer themselves as the antidote for your fear. They will come in and be the hero to rescue you from the fear. They might solve the problem they just caused for you, or they might give you the comfort you need to cope with the fear. Either way, they will show you that they can save you from your fears.

Once they have done this, they will try to make it appear that ONLY THEY can save you from your fears. They will try to show that others cannot protect you or solve the problem like they can. They will try to convince you that they are the only ones on Earth who can save you from your fears.

At this point, they own you. You might not even realize it yet, but they own you. It is very similar to a drug dealer giving away free drugs to create an addiction. Once they have you addicted, you will be forced to become a great on-going customer for them. It's the same with fear for the purpose of abuse. Once a person owns you, they can get you to do anything they want. You would find that you no longer have any power in whatever relationship or arrangement you are in.

At some point there is usually a test or a "reminder" of who is in control. The abuser will every once in a while, trigger you into fear, so that they can rescue you, so that you remember they are the only one who can save you, and that you NEED them. You can no longer function or live without them in your mind. You are absolutely dependent upon them, and they will remind you of this very often. You are officially under the control of another person and in an abusive situation.

How did this all start? This started because YOU HAD FEARS that an abuser was able to identify and then use against you. What is the solution to this problem? I'll give you ten seconds to think. Tick tock, tick tock, tick tock. TIMES UP. The solution to this problem

IS, that you eliminate your fears. If you eliminate your fears, then you will have no fears. If you have no fears, then there is nothing for an abuser to weaponize against you.

If you have no fear, you are pretty much immune from abuse. That does not mean people won't do mean or horrible things to you. Life is a battleground. It does not mean you will not have bad situations with bad people. But it means you will escape the figurative brawl bruised, but not defeated. Any abuser will see you cannot be controlled because they have nothing to manipulate you with, or control you with. Without some sort of mental weapon based upon fear, an abuser has nothing to use against you, and will move onto easier targets.

So now do you see why the weaponization of fear is far more terrifying than just being afraid to take an action or a chance at an opportunity? The latter just results on a one-on-one loss. But allowing fear to be weaponized against you by an abuser, allows another person to steal your life and own your life on an on-going basis with no expiration date. Fear being weaponized against you leaves you vulnerable 24/7 and will ruin your life. You will have no decent present or future under the control of someone using your fears against you.

This is why one of the most important CHANGES you will need to make is eliminating your fears so they can no longer be used against you. Hopefully you can see how powerful a person is who has no fears. It is critical for any warrior or person who wants to own themselves and be the master of their domain. Ascended Masters have no fear, thus being an advanced evolved person will mean having no fear.

Now let's be clear, having a fear of heights, snakes, or hot stoves is not what we are talking about here. Humans were first given fear as a tool of protection. Fear was a way to keep humans safe from harm. Fear is a learned response to danger. Fear is a reminder that something can harm us and we better be careful. This kind of fear is more of a physical response, rather than a mental response. This kind of fear can be helpful.

I am afraid of snakes because I don't want to be bitten. This is good for my health. You snake lovers can keep loving snakes. I know they play an important part in our eco-system. Each to their own. Others are afraid to walk alone outside at night in the dark. Is this an irrational fear of the dark? Or is this a helpful fear that prevents someone from being assaulted at night when it's not safe to be walking around alone? I am afraid to skydive out of an airplane with a parachute. Is this a fear I should eliminate? Or is this a valid fear of not wanting to take the chance of the parachute not opening? People who love jumping out of planes should keep doing it. But for others, the risk and stress are not worth it, however small the perceived risk. With that said, I can assure you that if my dream was to jump out of airplanes for the military, I would certainly face that fear and eliminate it. I am able to eliminate fears at will. You need to learn to do this also.

Here is the point I am trying to make. I really don't gain or lose much by my decision of deciding to play with snakes or not, or whether I jump out of planes or not. There is not much at stake with any fears related to those things, assuming they are not desired careers. Thus, I am not concerned about someone having those fears, or needing to eliminate those fears. It is not important in that context for them.

What I am concerned about are more EMOTIONAL PSYCHOLOGICAL fears. Fears such as death, being alone, failure, and such examples. Those are fears that can cause us to shut down, paralyze us, and cause us to stop taking actions and living our lives. If I fear snakes, I won't own a snake. But if I fear failure, I will likely not take any chances on anything at all. This means I stop living a productive life. The deeper more emotional fear of failure is the one we want to target and eliminate, not a fear of snakes.

51

Notice that I am using discernment here. There is no black or white absolute easy slogan to remember like many books out there. Similar to life, there are multi-layered complexities, and discernment must be used. I am hoping you see how I have distinguished between harmless fears and more harmful emotional fears that can be weaponized. If you want an easy sentence to remember, then maybe we can say, "If it is a fear that can be weaponized against you, then you must eliminate it." That phrase should work well most of the time. And yes, if my dream job ends up being one involving snakes, then I would then have to eliminate that fear, and I would. So yes, the phrase works. Just focus on the fears that can be weaponized against you or cause you to stop living life how you want.

The next obvious question and topic we need to cover is the solution of how we eliminate fears. It is easier said than done, right? Well, yes that is true. But it can be done if you are committed to doing the self-work necessary. Living without fear is a change we must make if we are to evolve.

First, you must realize that most fears are a result of an earlier trauma, event, or circumstance. It is possible that it's simply a result of what somebody said to you. Someone could have planted the fear within you without you having any direct experience with it. The first thing you must do is identify where your fear came from. It is easier if you take your fears one at a time. Thus, I am speaking in terms of each of your fears, not all your fears lumped together. You must ask, "why am I afraid of this?" Contemplate, and come up with some sort of answer.

Once you identify why you are afraid, you need to use logic, and try to show yourself how your fear is either entirely or partially illogical. Obviously, it is not logical to be afraid of dogs if one dog bit you 30 years ago. It might be time to realize that is illogical. It is not logical to be afraid of being alone simply because you have never been alone. How can you be afraid of it if you have never experienced it for a length of time? Or perhaps you were alone for a period in the past and it was horrible. You have to use logic to realize that just because it was horrible back then does not mean it would be horrible now or in the future, given different circumstances and age.

Or perhaps you are afraid of death. Well, it is not logical to be afraid of something that is not likely to happen now, but is absolutely going to happen eventually. Why be afraid of something that is certain, and something everyone will experience someday? You should ask yourself why you are afraid of death. Is there something specific about it that you fear? Is there something about how you are living your life that causes you to be uncomfortable with death? Are you not comfortable with your spiritual or religious beliefs to give you comfort? Why? There is much to examine. Death is an example of something everyone should become comfortable with, because everyone will experience it, and it frees you from a decaying body and allows you to continue your soul journey in a different form. I know this is a deeper topic, and requires deeper discussion, but you need to see that all fears need to be explored and faced. By the way, I have found that the fear of death is at the root of most fears. So, if you wanted the quick and harsh method of fear elimination, you could just focus on eliminating your fear of death first. Once you eliminate your fear of death, you will find most of your other fears just melt away and are gone.

Go through your inventory of fears, identify why you are afraid of each, and then realize your fear is illogical. After that, the next step is to EMBRACE your fear. Instead of looking away like before, look straight at it. Look at it good and close. Have a face-off. Look at your fear and say, "My fear of you was illogical." "What's the worst thing you can do to me, kill me?" "Well, I am not afraid of death, and I am not afraid of you." This is what I would say. Obviously if you are not that far along yet to be unafraid of death, you will have to back off from the strength of that statement. But you might say, "I am no

53

longer afraid of being alone because I know I would just keep living my life, and would be fine." This is an example of you actually imagining in your mind living out the fear, and realizing that the sun still rises in the morning and that life goes on. Remember, fears are irrational and illogical in most cases. Fears are like that monster in your head that tries to make you think you will be doomed, and life will end if you experience the consequence of the fear. It is critical you live out the fear in your mind to clearly see that life would go on. This is precisely why an abuser usually says, "You could never survive without me." They are trying to instill this sense of doom, and that life would end if you did not have them. In our process I have outlined, you would be able to see that life would go on. Life might change, but it would go on. Do not let abusers or fear place irrational consequences into your mind. They are false.

You need to fully face your fears and process them in your mind as if they have already happened. Once you process the worst-case scenarios, they become less scary. If your employer says, "If you leave my company, you will never work in this town again." Well, first of all, that is not logical and likely they cannot make that happen. But process the worst-case scenario anyway. Think about how what they are saying is just bluster, and even if they try to blacklist you with some companies, they cannot do it with everyone. Also, their blacklisting would likely not last long before everyone forgets what happened. Also, realize this horrible person likely has many enemies, and those enemies would likely love to hire you. There are so many ways I could go with this scenario. The bottom line is that this abuser's threat is nothing to be afraid of, and I would have a hard time containing my laughter as I am walking out the door.

What about a fear of failure? A person might be so afraid of failure that they are afraid to take a chance or try anything. This might stem from a failure early in life where parents or friends were disappointed in you or laughed at you as result of a failure or certain event. I would realize that it is irrational to fear something that happened long ago. I would also realize it is not logical to let other people's words dictate my actions and my future. Forget what happened in the past. It is not logical to be afraid for that reason. I would then face my failure by imagining that I would do if I take a chance and it fails. I would think, "Well, that sucks." But then I would realize that I would have learned a lot from the failure. Maybe if I could see why something failed, I could then try again a different way to prevent that failure from happening again. Maybe failing once is actually the key to success! "Wow, I can't wait to fail at this so that I can then try again doing it the correct way." I am not just being cheeky. I am being practical and real. Often times failure is one step closer to success. If you do not experience the failed steps first, you never get to the success. The sooner you get through those initial steps, the faster you will succeed. As with the other fears, EMBRACE failure. Be ready, prepared, and know some good will come from it. Welcome it and you will not be afraid of it. When you think of fearing failure, you will actually laugh instead. How's that for a CHANGE?

I am hoping you see a few things here. I am hoping you see how dangerous and destructive fear is. It will ruin your life if you don't defeat it. I am hoping you see how fear is used to manipulate and control you through abuse. I am hoping you see how you must eliminate fear and live your life without fear. Finally, I am hoping I gave you some perspective on how to defeat, eliminate, or at the least, set your fears aside. If you can live without fear, you are evolved.

CHAPTER SIX

Why Are Humans So Unhappy?

Not every human is unhappy. Some of you might be quite happy, and even delighted with life. I think that's great. That IS the goal, right? This chapter is not assuming you or everyone else is unhappy. This chapter is an exploration of why humans as a whole seem to struggle with unhappiness in general.

Most of us struggle to find happiness or remain in a happy state of mind. "Being happy" is kind of a sliding scale in more ways than one. Firstly, some are happy more often than others. Some might feel happiness most of the time, while others might only have brief moments of happiness on rare occasions. Furthermore, the intensity level of happiness is on a sliding scale. Happiness for some can be nearly orgasmic, while others view "happiness" as moments in time when they are not in absolute pain or misery. In other words, happiness for some is simply the absence of suffering, while others can soar up into the clouds with happiness. Any way you slice it, happiness is a good thing and something we all aspire to and can't get enough.

Even if you are happy, there is no disputing the growing epidemic of unhappiness among humans. All you need to do is look at the levels of depression, substance abuse, and suicides. Some people don't even know anyone who has not suffered from depression or substance abuse of some kind at some point in time. The levels of depression and substance abuse in our society seems to be increasing with time. Why is this? What can we do about this? How can we help YOU to be happier? Well, we will try to look for some answers.

When examining why humans tend to be unhappy, it is easiest to go back, way back, to the beginning of a human life. Let us go back to when a human is first brought into this world. A new baby is born. The first thing it does is cry. Why is this? Well apart from the natural reflex of clearing its lungs and getting everything working, the baby is cold and uncomfortable. It is a harsh world that is not a suitable environment for its comfort level. Bright lights and cold temperatures. The baby is immediately happier once it has been wrapped in a blanket. So, already this human has an issue with the environmental conditions here on Earth.

Next up, the baby has immediate needs. It is not long before the newborn is hungry. When it feels this hunger, it cries with discomfort and need. When a diaper change is required, it cries again with discomfort and need. In addition to the uncomfortable environmental factors, the baby is also faced with discomforts and needs for which it must depend on the whims of others.

It does not take long before the baby shows signs of preferring companionship. It likes to be held nearly all of the time. Babies do not like to be alone. New humans require companionship or they are very unhappy. Only sleep can give new parents a respite from the constant needs of a new child struggling to remain satisfied and happy in this new world.

As a baby turns into a toddler, the child is accustomed to certain routines, and has developed preferences of favorite activities to do and not do. If you try to change the routine, you will be met with a very unhappy child. If you do not allow the child to engage in favorite activities, you will see unhappiness at a tantrum level. If you try to engage the child in activities not liked, you will also see tantrum level unhappiness. Basically, if the little human is not allowed to follow its usual routine EXACTLY, or is not allowed to do exactly what it wants, when it wants to do it, OR is required to do anything not preferred, you will see a meltdown of great human proportions. OH, THE HUMANITY!

As our little new human ages, they become more self-reliant for basic needs, but they become no less willing to forsake activities they prefer, and become no more willing to partake in undesirable activities. The environment continues to be an issue, with specific needs for clothing, blankets, and indoor settings. Also, don't just assume ANY blanket will do. Oh no. It has to be a certain plushy blanket of a certain size, weight, and color, in order to satisfy this human. The human requirements never end!

I think you get my point, and I will spare all of us the great agonizing pain of having to discuss the teenage years. You're welcome. So, the original question was, "Why are humans so unhappy?" My answer is that humans were never happy. From the time a human is born, the environment is really not to their liking, there is a list of needs that can never be satisfied quickly enough, and there is an absolute inflexibility when it comes to routines, likes, and dislikes. Humans are very particular creatures who require great care and have no tolerance for any deviation away from their expectations of needs, wants, and desires. Humans are very delicate and difficult creatures. Exhausting.

These innate qualities tend not to get better with age. Yes, an adult MIGHT stop having tantrums in the middle of the grocery store. But we all know that these same adults will still have their tantrums in private by themselves, or with their significant partners and companions in life.

Let's examine more closely what causes adult humans so much unhappiness. One of the biggest is EXPECTATIONS. As with children, adults have certain expectations of things they expect(need) to happen, in addition to how they expect others to behave around them, and what others are expected (supposed) to do for them. A human develops this manufactured plan in their mind of how everything around them is SUPPOSED to go. You know, this person is supposed to do this, and then that person will do that, and then I can do this, and then my money will arrive on this day, which allows me to do something on that day, and of course the weather will have to be perfect on that day, and the birds must be singing, and everything will be fine. At least it better be fine or there will be hell to pay, the human thinks. And this is an ADULT thinking this. Is there really any difference between an adult and an infant? Does anyone see problems with this type of thinking? Yes, this might be laughable, but most of us are guilty of thinking this way.

We have such strict and specific EXPECTATIONS of how we think, what we want, and how we need things to proceed. When one or more of these pieces don't work out the way we had expected, we become unhappy. Then it is as if we are SHOCKED things did not work out as we planned. We are somehow surprised that ALL of our plans and expectations did not come to fruition exactly as we planned and wanted. Are we really that naïve and arrogant? Why yes, yes we are. We are humans after all! We expect to have things our way. It started when we were born and it continues today.

All I mentioned above seems bad enough, but it gets even

59

worse. For whatever reason, in recent decades humans have been building a society and world that is increasingly difficult to live in. The world has become incredibly competitive and demanding, to the point that failure at some level is nearly inevitable. What I mean by that is our children are in a rat race, having to score at a certain level on certain tests on certain days, or their chosen future path may be unavailable to them in terms of schooling. Hard working people are losing their jobs at the whim of corporate consolidations and other considerations that are far outside our control, and even far outside the control of their immediate supervisors and those who actually work with them. It is difficult to get affordable high quality health care depending on your circumstances and where you live. Everything is so expensive that it can become impossible to stay afloat. It just seems that the limitations are increasing, and benefits are decreasing. The pressure is sometimes more than a person can handle.

What I am describing is a very harsh, difficult, and even somewhat impossible environment in which humans must operate. May I remind you that humans are delicate creatures that do not do well in situations where they don't get to do things they enjoy. It is as if humans have somehow built the exact world they would dislike the most. This is perhaps a great theme for another book. For now, let's stick to how humans can navigate this situation in a struggle to find happiness.

It might all seem hopeless, but it's not. There are things people can do to evolve beyond some of the limitations that are keeping them stuck in a state of unhappiness. However, the bad news is that it requires one thing very important. Change. Maybe some of you saw that coming?

Let's go back to basics and look at the human attributes that are most at fault in causing the problems. Those would be expectations and inflexibility. Humans have all their expectations they manufacture and must be met. Furthermore, humans love their fixed routines and are inflexible regarding them most of the time. These human traits are mostly to blame for our constant disappointment and frustrations that can cause our unhappiness.

The answer is somewhat obvious I suppose. In order to decrease our level of unhappiness in such a harsh difficult world, we need to evolve by making changes to those two attributes mentioned. It would be a big step to think we can totally eliminate those two attributes causing our weakness. Due to that, we won't have such high "expectations" of totally eliminating those at this point. Let us instead focus on turning down the dial of those attributes in order to mitigate their effect upon us.

We must decrease or stop our constant expectations of almost every person, and every thing, in our little worlds. Stop making constant assumptions. Stop assuming that everyone is going to do what they said they would do. Stop expecting people to do things at the time they said they would do them. Stop expecting your plans to work out as planned. THEY WON'T. Remember that External Forces are always very strong and will always interrupt your plans. If you want to expect something, then expect that your plans are not going to go as planned. You will end up being correct about that expectation most of the time, if not always.

Expect the unexpected. Expect disappointments. Expect some setbacks and failures. Expect some of the people around you to not perform as expected. Think of it this way. If you let go of all your expectations, you would not be surprised or disappointed nearly as often. You would simply observe the outcome of a situation, and then you could quickly and efficiently react to that situation without anger and frustration for your expectations being broken.

Increase your level of flexibility. Accept ahead of time that you WILL have to adjust and CHANGE. If you factor in that you will have to make changes in plans, it makes it easier to see unexpected results and then adjust to them. A true Master can adjust to any situation. Instead of going through life expecting and hoping everything will go as you want and expect, you should go through life expecting and embracing the adjustments you will have to make. You won't know what those adjustments are until the situation arises, but you will know for certain that you will have to make adjustments. Be flexible enough to anticipate and embrace adjustments to your plans and your thinking.

I realize you might have been EXPECTING me to give some easy solution on how you can be happy 100% of the time. Sorry if I did not meet your EXPECTATIONS. However, I have pointed out hard facts of life and human psychology. Like with most things, the answers you are seeking ARE available, but they are found within the reality of hard work. Other books might have told you of an affirmation to say every morning that would make you happy forever. People love those books. They make everything sound so easy, and they give you everything you are hoping to hear. Of course, they don't actually work. But it doesn't stop people from wanting to believe. I am not telling you to stop believing. I am just suggesting that you realize all the answers are found within the reality of facts, human psychology, and your own imagination for evolving.

Your ability to evolve is the magic you are seeking. It can change everything for you. It is this magic I am trying to show you. Yes, this magic can even help you find happiness if you are willing to change and do the work. You and your ability to evolve is magical, and that should give us all great happiness.

CHAPTER SEVEN

Perception

Some say that "reality is a matter of perception." Umm no. Reality is REALITY. Your perception of reality is only YOUR perception. And YOUR perception does not change REALITY. Humans can be arrogant creatures and they THINK that whatever they THINK is what things are, or are what they want them to be, or can make them into anything they want them to be just by thinking it. This is arrogance and shows a lack of emotional maturity, not to mention a logical awareness. An evolved human becomes more adept at recognizing true REALITY, and what their role in it may or may not be. Humans can choose to live IN TRUTH, or humans can choose to live in some sort of delusional false alternative dimension that is a result of THEIR PERCEPTION.

A person's perception of situations is very often faulty. If you are basing your decisions and reactions upon a faulty perception, then that will give you a very bad result. I view mistakes in perception to be a form of self-sabotage. I say this because from an objective point of view, it often seems that a person is very reckless with their perception of a situation. It is almost as if they don't put any care or thought into how they perceive a certain situation. Thus, when their reaction or choice is wrong, it seems it was a totally needless negative outcome that could have been avoided if they took more care in basing their choices on a more accurate perception from the beginning.

Because people end up with so many problems and bad results from these reckless inaccurate perceptions, it really is necessary to change how a person perceives things if one is to evolve. Let us explore this area of human behavior in hopes we can gain a better "perception," resulting in less problems and better outcomes.

Humans tend to view life through a very limited lens from the point of view of "self." Their perceptions are usually formed only by their own personal experiences, opinions, knowledge, desires, anger, frustrations, fears, and other personal emotional factors. How else should their perception be based you may ask? Well, ideally a person's perception would be based upon the totality of REALITY. The totality of reality is like viewing the entire Universe, while a normal perception from the view of limited "self" is like viewing life by what you can see within one room of your house.

My example of viewing life by what you can see in one room of your house is almost literal. There ARE people whose perceptions are based solely on their own existence within their home. They might not get out much. Perhaps they are not very social and do not have much contact with the outside world. These people will eventually begin to only see life through their daily lens within their very tiny limited universe of life. Based upon such a small view of reality, just imagine how they might perceive different situations, and imagine how accurate their perceptions of life would be.

My grandmother, God rest her soul, was a lady I really enjoyed. She drove my mother absolutely crazy. This might be one of the reasons I really enjoyed her. But she and I got along perfectly, and I feel I understood her frustrations, even at a very young age. She had stories to tell that I never heard from my mother or anyone else. Plus, she served me ice cream with *Magic Shell* chocolate covering. Anyways, my grandmother lived alone and did not get out much. When my mother and I used to go over and visit her, she would tell us about all the things in life that annoyed her. I would smile with amusement while my mother sighed and braced herself for patience.

My grandmother used to complain because her neighbors would start their cars early in the morning. My grandmother liked to stay up late and sleep late. So, when the neighbors would start their cars outside her bedroom window early in the morning, it would disturb my grandmother's sleep. She used to claim that the neighbors were doing it on purpose to annoy her. She perceived the neighbors as being annoying, and purposely wanting to annoy her by INSISTING they start their cars every morning "on purpose." She was absolutely convinced they hated her and wanted to make her life miserable just for something to do because they had nothing else to do. My mother and I would look at each other and laugh. My mother would say, "Well did you ever consider that they were starting their cars to go to work each morning like everyone else?" My grandmother would just pause and there would be this blank space in the conversation, then she would continue on with her complaints.

You see, my grandmother had this perception that a certain major annoyance of hers was purposely targeted and aimed at her by others. She felt it was about her, and it was a purposeful attack upon her by the neighbors. Her perception was based upon her own reality of not working and never needing to leave the house early in the morning. Not a single morsel of her perception was based upon anything outside her little reality of her home and her own routines. Thus, this created a perception so incorrect that it was comical.

This may be an extreme example, but it serves to show how a person with a very limited perception can have a very inaccurate and distorted view of reality. Most humans to some degree have a distorted view of reality because of a limited or inaccurate perception.

We have all had experiences where someone looked at us in a mean way, or said something that seemed mean. We naturally assumed that person must not like us, or has it out for us. We all have been in this situation, to later realize the person had nothing against us at all. Perhaps the person was having a really bad day or bad moment. Perhaps the person said something by mistake in a way they did not intend for it to be taken. I have certainly done this before to other people. I have said something in a very fast and stern way because I was very busy and I was trying to be succinct and efficient. However, the other person perceived it as me being rude or mean to them, or perhaps that I didn't like them.

We all have endless examples of misperceptions. The problem is that these misperceptions can do a lot of damage. They can hurt our careers, personal relationships, and give us a warped sense of reality that cause us to make weird and wrong decisions. Evolving into a greater person who enjoys better outcomes in life would most certainly require a change in how we perceive things. After all, many a salesperson has said, "Perception is everything."

So how do we change our perceptions? Well, the first step involves us recognizing that our current perceptions are flawed. They are based on a very limited lens from the perspective of "self," and they are usually based upon emotional factors and moods. We must CHANGE this basis for our perceptions.

I would suggest that our new basis for perceptions should be based upon a wider view of reality, outside our own selves, AND be based more upon logic rather than our emotions and moods. This, of course, is much harder to do than it sounds. Why is it so difficult? Because we are human. Well, most of us are anyway. But part of evolving is to do the difficult work of moving away from those easily flawed instincts, and into a more advanced and efficient method or manner.

How you achieve this change is by practice. Perceptions of situations come up constantly, so you will not have to wait long before you have opportunities to put this new thinking to the test. My suggestion is that whenever you see and feel a situation that might have a complex perception, that you slow it down and examine it carefully.

Ask yourself some questions.

1. Is my perception of this situation based upon an opinion, or facts and reality?
2. Is my perception of this situation based solely upon my own views only, or is it based upon multiple viewpoints of the other person, as well as neutral third parties?
3. Is my perception of this situation based upon my current mood and emotions, or is it based upon logic?

Asking yourself those three questions is a fast and easy way to interrupt your process of automatic assumptions and jumping to a false perception. Yes, there are times when if it walks like a duck and quacks like a duck, it IS a duck, and no further examination is needed. But in more than half of your situations, you will find the perception is more complicated than that. The three questions help prevent you from making automatic assumptions and jumping to conclusions that are wrong.

This is a skill that is not just used in your personal interactions and relationships, but can also be used in business. I teach people who are engaged in sales or have service clients to use this approach. The example is always that the business person loses a client and receives an email from the client that is very mean and nasty, and includes a termination at the end. Very often the business person will naturally assume something went very wrong, the customer hates them now, and perhaps it is best to just leave it alone. However, I advise the opposite. Instead of taking the assumed perception that the customer now hates you and will never do business again, the business person should instead not make such false perceptions that are not grounded in proven fact or reality. Instead, contact the customer. Find out exactly what happened. More times than not, it was some minor infringement that the customer interpreted as a major act of war. For example, a service worker might have tracked dirt onto their brand-new carpet they had installed one week prior. The service worker was not even thinking, the business owner was not even aware, but the customer got so angry that steam was coming out of their ears and their head was spinning off their shoulders. This would have resulted in the customer writing a hate-filled rant ending in a termination of services. Once you learn the true reason for the situation, you can have a new perception based upon REALITY AND FACTS. You can realize that the customer does not hate you and had no problem with the specific service. Instead, the problem was with a stupid act of tracking dirt onto a new carpet. Fully sympathize and empathize with the customer. Get angry WITH them. Offer to clean it. Tell them how you understand how they feel and that you valued their business way too much to just let them walk away with no explanation. Not only will you keep the customer, but you might get additional work from them in addition to referrals.

This type of thinking can work equally well in your personal life. When you see someone may have misperceived something, you should not make any misperceptions yourself about the situation. Instead, seek out the true facts and reality in a logical fashion so you can have an accurate perception of the situation. Then you can transfer this accurate perception over to the person who had the original misperception involving you.

I hope it is clear that you see it is critical to not only have accurate perceptions yourself, but to also help any opposing parties gain more accurate perceptions. It is a way of dispute resolution. People have careers based upon this ability to have accurate perceptions, and repair inaccurate perceptions. It's called human resources, sales management, outside sales, general management, and almost every other position you can think of that involves multiple people.

All of this translates equally in your personal life with your personal relationships. It also transfers into your own self-view of things. If my grandmother had used this approach, she would have quickly realized that if her neighbors need to get to work, then it means they need to start their cars, and that maybe it is not an offense against her after all. I ask my grandmother for forgiveness in using this example, but the truth is that we are ALL guilty of this kind of thinking from time to time. Why? Because humans simply have a natural tendency to make all perceptions based upon our own limited self-view that is based upon moods and emotions. It's that simple, and that brings us full circle.

So how do we proceed from now on? We make our perceptions based upon the true facts of reality from all perspectives, not just our own. We also use logic rather than our current mood and emotions. If we are able to make this change in how we base our perceptions, we will be one step further on our journey of becoming more evolved.

CHAPTER EIGHT

False Thinking

What do I mean by "false thinking?" For our purposes in this chapter, false thinking is reasoning that is based on false premises, false facts, illogical thinking, or conclusions that are based upon a false narrative. Let's see if I can come up with some stupid examples to help clarify this, or perhaps it will only make it more muddy. We shall see.

Someone might say they will not swim at a certain beach because they had a friend tell them they heard there was a shark in the area. This is false thinking for a couple reasons. First, it is based upon hearsay, which is indirect information from a witness that we cannot even identify. It was not even the friend who saw the shark, but rather a friend of a friend. Thus, we can't even identify that the source of the information even exists, let alone is credible. Furthermore, even if the witness and information was real, we don't know exactly when this happened. It could have happened ten years ago, or yesterday. When it happened matters in this situation. The result is that a person will not swim at a beach based upon useless anecdotal unconfirmed information from an unknown source with no time reference. If you were concerned about this matter, you could call the lifeguard public safety department. End of story.

Here is another example. Someone might say a certain new camera they have is horrible and faulty because they cannot even get it to work. This statement alone, with no other specific details, is faulty thinking. Why? Well, firstly, we know it's a new camera. If it is a new camera, it's likely not broken, and it likely needs to be set up by someone who knows something about cameras. A camera is not faulty or horrible just because the user is not knowledgeable enough to know how to use it. It might be the most advanced, greatest camera that ever existed. That would actually explain why the person has trouble getting it to work, if they don't have much experience with advanced cameras. Therefore, assuming it's horrible and faulty is not only false thinking, but the opposite of what they are saying might be the actual truth.

Let's try again. Someone might say that every January 27th, a flying saucer lands in their back yard and a unicorn walks down the ramp and runs off into the forest. Normally, nobody would believe this, but they produce a video on the internet with some grainy footage showing some kind of saucer landing, and then a separate shot of some kind of horse with something strapped to his head coming out of a machine and then running off. There will be people claiming this really happened because the video footage is "proof." Well, we all know some crazy video on the internet does not prove anything, right? Right??? Please tell me you agree with this. If you DO think it's proof, maybe don't say anything, and let's just move on. But clearly, providing "proof" of something that is not actually proof of something is false thinking. Just because someone says they have proof does not mean they have proof.

I am hoping you have an idea now what I mean by false thinking. It is basically coming to a false conclusion by using a flawed line of reasoning. The reasoning is flawed because it is based on untruths, weak assumptions, illogical assumptions, or fake and unproven evidence.

Sometimes false thinking is very simple and clear, as in the examples I gave above. Other times, false thinking is much more difficult to discern. Conspiracy theories are an excellent example of false thinking that is sometimes more difficult to identify as such, or perhaps it is truth after all. The reason some false thinking is difficult to discern is because some false lines of thinking contain morsels of proven factual truth. Someone might say, "I know that man stole my money because one year ago he stole my neighbor's money." That statement seems pretty solid. The reason it seems solid is because we will take it as a proven fact that one year ago the man stole from the neighbor. Fact. So, it is easy to jump to the conclusion that he was the thief in the most recent incident also. The only problem is that there is no proof of this. It is false thinking to absolutely assume someone did something today just because they did something similar a year ago.

If you look at all conspiracy theories, they all contain at least one piece of absolute truth. The proponents of the conspiracy theory provide this one kernel of truth as their PROOF that their convoluted theory is true. But of course, the conspiracy always has many issues preventing it from being real. Most of all, one small kernel of truth does not prove or validate all of the convoluted ASSUMPTIONS surrounding the one kernel of truth. The proponent would still need to provide factual evidence that does not include hearsay evidence of some unknown person, or some video on the internet showing someone saying the theory is true. A video having someone saying

72

that something is true is not proof of anything. Made up graphics or photos are not proof of anything either. One great way to know that something is a conspiracy theory and not real, is when you consider how it would do, or has done, in a court of law where absolute proof, facts, and real witnesses are required. Many conspiracy theories cannot even make it into a courtroom because they completely lack all of the components I just mentioned. Therefore, it is false thinking.

Some people might say, "Just because I am paranoid does not mean someone is not following me." Meaning, even if you think I am a kook, that does not mean I am wrong in what I say. That is true. To assume someone is wrong just because what they say sounds crazy, would be false thinking. If you can't prove what they are saying is wrong, then they COULD be right. But if you can't prove what they are saying is true, then they could be wrong also. A clear thinker is open to BOTH possibilities.

Why is any of this remotely interesting or even important? Well, it may or may not be remotely interesting, BUT, it is certainly very important. People who go through life using false thinking will always come to wrong conclusions. If they always come to wrong conclusions, then they will make bad decisions based upon wrong information. This causes problems in people's lives and does not help them progress, advance, or live a better life. If a person is to evolve, they must change, and stop using false thinking. Once you no longer use false thinking, you will find that you have much better clarity in life, and that you are making much better decisions that have a much better outcome.

How do we stop engaging with false thinking? The most important step is to use logic. Also, a great tool is to pretend you are a judge in a court of law. If you were a judge, what would you require to reason through something? Well, you would require facts, evidence, actual witnesses, and ultimately real proof. You would not get confused or distracted by one kernel of truth wrapped with all kinds of false assumptions. You would not accept an internet video of some guy saying something is true as the "proof" that something is true. You would not accept some unknown photo that might be photoshopped as proof of anything. You would use logic and common sense.

If someone is telling me something, I listen to them carefully. I listen for things they saw or experienced themselves, vs. something they heard from a friend or read someplace. I listen for facts and events that can be verified and proven. I listen for anything that might violate basic principles of mathematics and science. I don't accept any kind of weird sketchy "proof" that is not actually proof. In other words, I am a cynical judge sitting at a trial. I am thinking clearly and logically. I don't let shiny objects take my eye off the ball. I don't get detoured. As a matter of fact, much to people's annoyance, whenever I am personally in such a situation, I will often ask a person to backup or start over with their story if I see a gap or something illogical in what they are telling me. I explain that I need them to tell their story in a way that I can understand it, and that way is for the story to be told clearly, step by step, from the beginning to the end. This way I cannot be confused or get lost in some fog of trickery. I am the guy you never want at a magic show. I will be watching everything closely, and if I feel I was distracted for even a second, I will ask them to stop and start over. It is always those moments of distraction that the magician does their magic. Sorry kids, but yes, the secret to being a magician is creating those key moments of distraction. It's done all the time, including in sales, but I digress.

It is very important to use slow, clear, methodical, and logical thinking at all times when trying to discern a situation. If you don't do this, your chances of falling into false thinking are greatly increased. Avoiding false thinking takes a lot of practice. Detectives and judges do not become good at their job overnight. It takes them years of training and experience before these skills become second nature to them. You will have to practice them as well.

Before I move on though, I want to cover the converse situation of needing to be cynical. It would also be false thinking if you are TOO CYNICAL, and do not leave your mind open to possibilities. Let us say I said to you that aliens exist. You might ask me how I know this. I might tell you that I feel I have had contact with them, or even might have been abducted. I might even tell you some stories of what happened to me. Should you believe me, or not believe me? Which answer would be the one with false thinking?

Sorry, but it's a trick question. The correct answer is that you don't know. I made an assertion that sounds ridiculous and I offer no verifiable proof. But on the other hand, I made an assertion that cannot be disproven. Thus, you don't know what to think. Some people might look at me and think I am crazy and assume that what I am saying is false. Other people might listen to my stories, look at me in my totality, and think I am credible and believe my assertions. But either way, I cannot prove my assertions, nor can they be disproven. Therefore, the correct course of action would be for you to listen carefully, take it all in, and realize that YOU DON'T KNOW THE TRUTH of this situation. In this instance, you would simply not fully believe, but you would also leave your mind open to the possibility it is true. THIS type of thinking is where we want to end up. We want to get to a place in our minds and thinking where we cannot be fooled into believing false things, BUT we also will not close our minds off to things that COULD be true, because there is no evidence proving it can't be true. This would be an evolved person who won't be easily fooled on the one hand, but is ready and willing to accept new advanced concepts on the other hand.

There are many things in life that seem absolutely impossible and unreal until we experience them ourselves. Then, once we see that the impossible is possible, our view of reality changes, but of course those around us will still not believe because it is still impossible in their view. This is okay. Do not expect them to believe you. But also hope

75

that they would have an open mind if it cannot be disproven.

Usually when people ask me a direct question, they expect a direct answer from me. However, there are times when my answer is, "I don't know." I use that answer in all fairness when I cannot prove or disprove. If I were to just guess and choose the obvious assumption, I would not be living up to what I am preaching in this chapter. Therefore, out of fairness and truth, I will sometimes say "I don't know," when I feel choosing one assumption or another will lead to false thinking. I would rather not know the answer than be certain of an answer using false thinking. Being evolved does not mean you know everything. It just means you know how to think in an evolved way.

CHAPTER NINE

The Law Of
Attraction?

I cannot have a chapter on false thinking and not have a discussion about The Law of Attraction. First, I want to say that I realize my thoughts on this subject may be unpopular with some. Not everyone will agree with me, and I think that is totally fine. Also, there are good parts and bad parts to most things. The Law of Attraction is no exception to this rule. I am sure some feel they have benefited from some of its principles. I am also sure many have been disappointed, and many more indoctrinated into a false delusion of false thinking from The Law of Attraction.

The Law of Attraction is a belief that your thoughts, and what you manifest into your life, are mirror images of each other. Or in other words, you attract into your life what you think. Or how you think dictates what manifests into your life. For example, positive thoughts will manifest positive things into your life, just as negative thoughts will manifest negative things into your life. I will also give The Law of Attraction the benefit of the doubt in all fairness, and add that some ACTIONS on your part are also required for The Law of Attraction to work.

This way of thinking, belief, cult, has sold billions of dollars worth of books, audio programs, videos, training programs, and live event performances. Millions of people became true believers. I'm sure some of you are among them. Again, I am not striving to invalidate your core beliefs. I am just presenting information, thoughts, and beliefs as I see them. You can take on board what serves you, and leave the rest. But I would be untrue to myself, my work, and my beliefs, if I did not raise the issues regarding this brand of thinking known as The Law of Attraction.

First, let me say that I do not think there is any harm in thinking positive thoughts. In fact, I believe it is helpful to think positive thoughts. I also think it is helpful to have your thoughts (and actions) in positive alignment with the goals and results you are trying to manifest or achieve. So far, so good, yes? Maybe I am a believer in The Law of Attraction after all? Or, maybe not so much.

I do not believe the Universe is so simple and easy that a human can think a positive thought of something they want, and it magically appears. Sorry, call me cynical. I am likely not a good choice to invite to someone's party. I might pop the balloons, or perhaps poke holes in people's delusions. I am very realistic and I live in truth. I do not engage in false thinking, although I am open to possibilities. I am very realistic and know the facts and truth of reality are not always super exciting and happy. I know that a human thinking a positive thought will not give them whatever they seek. I hope I didn't just crush all your hopes and dreams.

Let's use our new skills regarding false thinking. The Law of Attraction proponents will often cite individual examples of people who thought a positive happy thought about something they wanted, and then received what they wanted. That sounds pretty convincing, doesn't it? It is VERY CONVINCING in a video or a live performance. So what we have is a kernel of absolute truth. Let us assume the person did indeed think the positive thought and then did indeed receive what they were trying to manifest. It did actually happen. The Law of Attraction worked for them. That is a fact. I take that as evidence. HOWEVER, the conclusion that if it worked for them means it will work for you and everyone else in the world, is a false conclusion. For that one success story, there are multiple times more who did not have happy good things happen to them as a result of their positive thinking. Thus, it is false thinking to say that a few individual success stories PROVE that The Law of Attraction works.

Let's change perspectives and look at it more logically. If it is true that good things come to those who think positively, then mathematically it MUST be true that bad things happen to those who think negatively. Also, it MUST hold true that EVERYONE who thinks positive thoughts get their positive results, not just a few lucky examples. Equations have two sides and both sides must balance out. Logic and math have been employed, therefore I'm afraid false thinking will have to step down and have a seat.

You cannot have a "universal theory" that works a few times, but not many other times. You can't just pick and choose what examples to use. We must take all the evidence, including the favorable and the unfavorable. I know that is not any fun and I just popped all your balloons. But it's reality.

I think we all know from personal experience that we can think the most positive thoughts of any human alive, but sometimes things don't work out well for us. It's a reality of life. That in itself is evidence that

79

The Law of Attraction does not work. Proponents might double-down and say that we were mistaken and that our thoughts were not actually positive, even though we just said they were positive. Or, maybe we need to buy more books to learn how to make our thoughts MORE positive, and we will get better results. Phooey.

What does The Law of Attraction say about innocent little children who get cancer? Did they have negative thoughts that brought that negative force into their life? Is their cancer actually their fault because of their thoughts? According to The Law of Attraction, yes. But again, proponents would dismiss this example as "horrible and not relevant," and would change the subject. Some might even say that The Law of Attraction does not pertain to negative outcomes like this, but only positive outcomes. Sigh. Eye roll. Phooey again. We know logically and mathematically that there are two sides to an equation, and if the positive gives a result, then the negative must also give a result. You cannot pick and choose what pieces of thought you accept, and which parts you pretend do not exist because they don't fit your desired narrative.

What about soldiers who get shot or step on landmines? Could that have been avoided if they had more positive thoughts? Do you see now how this type of thinking can actually be offensive? Essentially, The Law of Attraction belief system actually blames people for the bad things in their life, as if their thoughts were not positive enough. If only you read more motivational books and controlled your positive thoughts better, horrible things would not have happened to you. But you didn't buy enough books, so your horrible events are your fault. If you didn't achieve your goals, it must be because you failed at thinking positive thoughts. All of this is offensive to me personally, but again, each to their own beliefs. I am fine with others disagreeing with me and having different beliefs. We can all still get along and be friends.

In summary, I don't believe The Law of Attraction is valid. I believe it is false thinking. I believe there are some limited examples where people who thought positive thoughts received what they wanted. That is not proof, and I laid out examples and reasons why it doesn't work. But then again, I have not made any money off of The Law of Attraction, so maybe I am just cranky and full of sour grapes.

My goal in this chapter is not to rain on the parade of everyone who is making money off The Law of Attraction. I am also not trying to change your core belief system if you feel The Law of Attraction is the reason you were able to buy that Mercedes you wanted. My goal is to help people evolve from false thinking. Thus, I was forced to discuss The Law of Attraction, because, well, it's false thinking. Need I say more?

Additionally, I am not one to say an idea won't work, and then leave the room without providing an alternative that does work. I am not trolling The Law of Attraction. I am simply pointing out facts and flaws. With that said, I believe I have developed a much more accurate, realistic, and truthful model for manifesting goals into your life. It is called the Hunter Equation.

I first developed this equation theory in my book by the same name, *The Hunter Equation*. I have also laid out the theory in my books, *Rising To Greatness* and *Heal Me*. From here on forward, when I say "the Hunter Equation," I am not talking about the book, but rather talking about the actual equation. The Hunter Equation states:

FUTURE OUTCOME = (INTENT + ACTIONS + EXTERNAL FORCES + RANDOM LUCK)

As you can see, the Hunter Equation includes four elements in the determination or manifestation of your Future Outcome or desired goal. The first element is indeed The Law of Attraction element of "Intent," or in other words, "positive thought," which we will give The Law of Attraction full credit for. The second element is "Actions," which we also decided to give The Law of Attraction the benefit of the doubt, and say it promoted that element as well. However, the Hunter

Equation adds the additional elements of "External Forces" and "Random Luck" to the life equation. For clarity's sake, I am going explain each of the elements so we are very clear on how this equation works.

FUTURE OUTCOME - Your FUTURE OUTCOME is obviously your results. It can also be your goal. So, if you had a goal you were trying to reach or achieve, you would put the goal or desired outcome into the equation as the Future Outcome. The Future Outcome can also be the unintended result of what you received.

INTENT - The INTENT is your intention and attitude. If you understand The Law of Attraction, then you understand what the Intent is. Intent means the same here as it does with The Law of Attraction. Intent is what you are intending, and your attitude toward your intention.

ACTIONS - The ACTIONS are exactly what you think they are. These are the steps or actions you are taking to achieve your goal or result. Actions can be positive, negative, or neutral. Actions are simply what you are actually doing.

EXTERNAL FORCES - This is the first new element I introduced, and likely the most important. EXTERNAL FORCES are all of the things that can happen outside of your control. We do not directly control External Forces. We do not live in a vacuum, and sometimes things surrounding us affect us. Sometimes it does not matter how positive your thoughts and attitudes are, bad things can still happen to you, or we get results we did not anticipate or intend. An example of an External Force would be when we are doing a great job at work, the boss loves us, we have a great attitude, great thoughts, and everything is going great; but then the company gets bought-out, and you get fired because of the restructuring. That is an External Force. You have no control over it, and there is nothing you could have done to avoid it. Life happens. Conversely, your boss giving you an unexpected raise can also be an External Force because it was mostly outside of your control and not anticipated, yet it will have a major impact on your situation. Plenty of times, good things happen to people even if they were not intending or trying for them. Health issues outside our control are other External Forces. Things that happen to our family members that directly change our own lives are External Forces. So much of how life turns out for us is a result of External Forces. It does not matter how great your thoughts and attitudes are. THIS is the reason I think The Law of Attraction can be a bit narcissistic and gaslight you. The Law of Attraction might say that you somehow could have avoided bad things happening to you if you had a more positive outlook, thoughts, intentions, or what have you. But we can clearly see there are plenty of instances where bad things happen completely outside our control, regardless of how positive our thoughts were. Basically, The Law of Attraction will blame you for your misfortune, saying it's your fault because of your thoughts, or even actions. Sometimes, things that happen to us are NOT our fault. MANY things are NOT in our control and are not our fault. Our thoughts are irrelevant in many cases. External Forces take this universal truth and reality into account. Any life theory that does not account for External Forces outside of our control is simply not based in reality.

RANDOM LUCK - This is the second "new" element I added. RANDOM LUCK is controversial because some people do not believe anything is random. Some people believe there is a reason for everything, and everything is based upon your DESTINY and pre-ordained design. I disagree fully. I believe that there is a random element in the Universe. If you put a bunch of jellybeans in a jar, close your eyes, reach in, and pull one out, was THAT jellybean randomly chosen, or was it pre-ordained that it would be chosen? Yes, some of you will argue with me until the end of time that the one jellybean you chose was meant to be chosen from the beginning of its existence. We will have to agree to disagree. Do you also believe every time you throw dice, that the outcome is pre-ordained? Do you believe when you flip a coin, that the coin has a destiny to land on one side or another? Do you believe that when you pick up a rock and throw it into a lake, that the specific rock you picked up was DESTINED to be chosen by you, and DESTINED to land in an exact spot out in the lake?

From a scientific point of view, I believe there is a random component because the Universe is always expanding, black holes changing, things growing, things dying, things being born. All of these natural organic changes ensure that there are constant VARIATIONS and VARIABLES in the Universe. These variables allow a random component to exist. But back down here to our reality, it just makes sense that some things are random.

To be honest, I explain all of this in much more detail and in-depth in *The Hunter Equation* book. I also give examples of how to use the equation in your life for making decisions and manifesting desired results. *Rising To Greatness* also does a good job at this. But I am hoping I have adequately made my case so that you will at least accept the possibility of a random component. In summary, Random Luck is the element that not only do we not control, but nobody controls it, except for the power of God and the Universe that allows it to exist, if you believe in those concepts.

In a nutshell, the Hunter Equation takes into account the useful parts of The Law of Attraction, but it adds the other real-world elements into the mix so that now there is a life equation that is more practical and truthful. Life is never simple or easy. Life is complex and full of surprises and problems. I believe my equation accounts for these complexities and surprises. It accounts for events that are outside of our control. These are events outside our control that a positive thought does not control. Oh, how I wish a positive thought would control all outcomes! I really do! But that is wishful thinking and not reality. That would be false thinking. We are not doing that anymore, as we are evolving.

CHAPTER TEN

Independent Thinker

Now that we covered false thinking, we have to move on to becoming more independent in our thinking. Humans are very easily influenced on how and what they think. "Peer pressure" is a good phrase to describe what I am trying to get at. That term also helps to support the fact that what many refer to as "group thinking" starts very early in childhood. Children tend to look toward their parents for direction on what to think. They mimic their parents and tend to adopt the same "talking points," opinions, and beliefs. As kids get older, they will adopt the beliefs of their friends and peers at school. As people grow into adults, they tend to adopt the thinking of their peer group, whether that be social or work. A person's type of thinking can also be formed based upon what news media they consume.

Humans will jump from peer group to peer group, in search of a belief system, or opinions, that they resonate with. A person's thinking is heavily influenced by their culture, family beliefs, where they live, and what they do for a living. Eventually, a person's views become very polarized to the point where they are no longer open to other viewpoints or types of thinking. Sadly, when you ask someone why they think the way they do, they often cannot answer the question. They may say, "Because I do," or they will engage in some false thinking to try and justify their thinking. People will often simply imitate phrases and words they heard others in their peer group or news media say. They may not even fully understand the meaning and context behind the phrases they use, but they don't care. People are most comfortable thinking the same way as their chosen peer group.

We have to parse our words carefully in this chapter. I do not want anyone to think it is wrong to have the same opinions as others in your peer group. Sharing an opinion that you have in common with others close to you makes plenty of sense. But here is the distinguishing factor. A person should be able to intelligently (without using false thinking) explain why they hold the opinions they do. If a person can INDEPENDENTLY explain and validate their thinking, then to me that is a valid opinion or way of thinking, whether you or I agree with them or not. HOWEVER, if a person is unable to explain their opinion and thinking, and only hold those thoughts because of others they know, then that is a person who is not thinking independently.

The inability or unwillingness to think independently is not only dangerous, but it will inhibit a person's potential for growth on many levels. It is dangerous because it means the person is open to brainwashing and mindlessly following a leader, regardless of the leader's intent. It inhibits a person's growth because ultimately, nobody is inspired by a parrot who just repeats and follows others, and has no original thoughts of their own.

If you look at human history and human evolution in general, there is a long history of "the masses" simply going along with whatever the "herd" is doing at the moment. The herd is usually led by one or a few leaders who actually make the consequential choices. The herd is conditioned, and conditions itself, to automatically agree with, and go along with, whatever the agenda set by the leader happens to be. It really does not matter how egregious, destructive, or stupid the agenda is. The herd will agree within itself that it is correct.

Why are humans like this? Why are humans so desperate to adopt the thinking and opinions of their peer groups? Are humans incapable of developing their own thoughts and opinions? Do humans actually NEED others to tell them what to think? I believe the answer is buried within our human culture and psychology. It is based upon human culture because humans from very early on in history survived by gathering into communities. "It takes a village" to accomplish many things.

Humans need food, shelter, medical care, education, and spiritual guidance in most cases. There is usually not a single person who can do ALL of these things. Therefore, humans joined communities where there were enough people with different skill-sets to fulfill all of these basic functions. Some members were really good at hunting and provided the food for everyone. Others would have no chance at successfully hunting and obtaining food, but were really good at raising the young, or providing personal care or medical care. Elders who were too old to hunt or provide defense, would be very good at providing spiritual and mental guidance. Thus, you needed a community in order to receive all the services required for survival.

Here is the hitch. In order to exist in this community in a harmonious way, everyone had to agree on basic principles and values. They could not have people in the community causing disruption and problems because of large disagreements of opinion. Therefore, it became a social norm that everyone in that community would share common beliefs and think the same way. This would result in a peaceful, productive, harmonious community. In other words, you either sign onto that community's norms, beliefs, and thinking, or you leave. Back then, leaving likely meant death. That's quite an incentive to stay.

I also mentioned human psychology as a reason people tend not to think independently. What I mean here is that the human psyche likes to have validation and approval from those around them. Most humans find it difficult to be the lone person with the different opinion or thinking from everyone else around them. Humans are very uncomfortable being socially and intellectually isolated. A person would rather be wrong and included, than be correct and excluded. That really is the bottom line right there. A person's need to be liked, included, validated, and approved, is FAR MORE IMPORTANT than a person's desire to give a correct assessment, even if that assessment is a work of genius and accuracy.

In too many cases, a person has no problem being completely wrong, or even immoral, as long as their "community" accepts them. The human psyche really craves and needs that acceptance from others. Without acceptance from others, people feel too uncomfortable, sad, insecure, and isolated.

After my explanations I think you can see why most people not only do not engage in independent thinking, but do not even want to, even if they could. People just prefer to keep holding the thoughts of their peer group, even if those beliefs make no sense, are incorrect, or are morally questionable, or worse.

So why am I writing this chapter? Why would we discuss something that most people have no interest in changing or developing? The reason is that this book is about evolving. Evolving means changing. Evolving means growing and developing into more than what we are today. Even if many people don't see a need or desire to change today, it does not make it any less valid or important. As some people choose to evolve, they will inevitably have to accept that "group think" needs to be left behind, and independent thinking must be embraced.

What are the benefits of independent thinking? First of all, we can avoid the dangerous effects of the masses following delusional, dangerous, and destructive leaders or community policies. When people value making the right choice instead of the peer group choice, we then have a system of checks and balances that can prevent violence, loss, and even war. That reason alone is enough justification to feel a sense of relief when people no longer automatically agree with the herd.

Additionally, independent thinking fosters more innovation, great ideas, and new ideas. When people automatically follow the herd style of thinking, they are not really thinking. They are just robots following the programming of those around them. Without any deep introspective and questioning thought, it is not as likely they will come up with new out-of-the-box ideas. You cannot think out-of-the-box when you have sealed yourself up inside the box. Independent thinking allows for new ideas and perspectives that will result in the evolution of not only that person, but also the community that person contributes to. It should be noted that independent thinking does not mean you have to live isolated with no friends or community. All that is required is for the community norms to start accepting independent thought.

Some might ask why we need to change things after humans have lived this way, and have been thinking this way, for so long. Well, let me refer you back to why "group think" started in the first place. It started because way back in time humans could not survive unless they joined a community. It was the only way to literally have food, shelter, and care. Therefore, there was little choice if a person wanted to survive.

I am not sure you noticed, but this is no longer the Stone Age. Human civilization has developed to the point that we don't

NEED to be living in a community in order to eat, live, and survive. We can pull in the resources, skills, and talents we need from the outside in any direction we choose. A person can be living in isolation in the middle of the forest and still get the services they truly need when they need them. Times have changed. Because civilization and technology has changed, humans have the license and opportunity now to disconnect from the old way of human thinking, and evolve into a more advanced independent way of thinking.

Next, you may ask how we can get this independent thinking stuff started. Do we just get up off our chair and start thinking independently? Is it that easy? No, it is not that easy. As with other things we are discussing in this book, some things take some time to understand it, digest it, and much practice is needed. But I can suggest ways to start on the path.

To begin, you must start from within. You must start to question what you think and why you think it. You can pick any of your opinions or positions in life. Ask yourself why you feel that way. A correct answer requires that you justify it with real facts and logical thinking. If your answer to your own question is "I don't know why I think this," or "I think this because such and such a person or group says it's true," then you have some work to do. At that point, you can engage in some research and introspective thought. Start to develop your own thoughts about the subject. You might find you partly agree, and partly disagree, with your previous opinions. This is what we are looking for and a sign you are making progress. We are not seeking for you to disavow all your prior beliefs. To the contrary. We are actually looking for you to confirm your beliefs, but with real justifications that do not blindly come from others. Most likely, you will find that you agree with some parts of beliefs, but not other parts. That is healthy. Doing this allows you to develop your own set of beliefs. By the time it's all over you might proclaim that you don't agree with ANYONE. You might find that your own beliefs do not match perfectly with ANY peer group. This is when you know you have reached the Promised Land of independent thinking.

Once you feel you are starting to feel it from within, you need to learn how to express it outwardly toward other people. This takes diplomacy. The purpose of independent thinking is not to start disagreements with everyone you know. Quite the opposite. With my approach, you should find yourself in LESS disagreements. How is this possible, you ask? Well, when a person states their position, your independent thinking mind should be listening carefully and taking it all in. Very often, you will agree with at least some small part of their thinking, even if you mostly disagree with their position as a whole. Your response to them should be something like, "While I don't entirely agree with what you just said, I do agree with parts of it, and you make some good points." Or you can say, "I agree with A, but I don't agree with B." Note that your response is not designed to say they are wrong or that you disagree. Your response is actually designed to find some common agreement anywhere you can possibly find it.

With your new independent thinking, you might find you have MORE friends, and can engage in conversations with all kinds of people who have very diverse opinions and beliefs. Independent thinking is not designed for disagreement or agreement. It is designed for you to keep an open mind and think very carefully and critically before deciding on your opinion. Independent thinking is designed to result in the type of thinking and reasoning that results in intelligent, thoughtful, factual, and innovative opinions, while avoiding false thinking and mindless opinions. Evolve your thinking to a whole new level with independent thinking, and become an independent thinker.

CHAPTER ELEVEN

Multi-Dimensional Thinking

We have done a lot of heavy lifting in this book so far. Mostly, we have focused on things that maybe have been broken and needed to be changed. Finally, we are making some progress and have begun to focus on items that we can further DEVELOP, rather than just "fix." I call that progress. First, we fix what's broken, and then we start to develop and grow. That's evolution.

Now that we have discussed how NOT to think (false thinking), and we have discussed how we SHOULD think (independently), we should proceed forward and discuss how we COULD be thinking. We could be, should be, and will be, using multi-dimensional thinking. Some of you may already be on your way to this, or engaging in it to some degree, but it's helpful to further explore the concept.

What do I mean by "multi-dimensional thinking?" Do I mean we need to think in terms of being on Earth, while at the same time thinking in the parallel dimension within the Vega Quadrant on the other side of space? No, I don't mean that. What I mean by "dimensions" is really "point of views."

For example, one dimension of thinking is single dimensional thinking in terms of "self." In one dimensional thinking, we are only thinking in terms of ourselves. What we want, what we need, what we feel. That is one dimensional thinking.

Two-dimensional thinking would be thinking in terms of "self" and "the other person." So, thinking two dimensionally means you are just thinking in terms of you and the other person you are engaging with. You might be thinking about what you want and need, and how you can get this from the other person from their perspective as well as your own. You might be speaking to them and trying to express your wants and needs, while sort of listening to them (but not really), and hoping to hear from them that you are convincing them with your argument. OR, you are listening for them to accept your argument, or to give a compromise. Either way, it is only about you and them.

Sadly, most people only think in one or two dimensions. This is based upon the fact that humans primarily operate from a motivation of NEED and WANT for themselves or immediate family. There are some humans that will literally only speak or communicate when they need or want something for themselves. This starts when we are babies. A baby will generally remain silent until they need or want something. Then they cry. Sometimes people act like babies for their entire lives. They will cry when they want or need something. Any way you slice it, one and two-dimensional thinking are rudimentary and we can do better.

Some of you may be wondering and asking what other "dimensions" could there be? This is not a stupid or embarrassing question. I know I just made two-dimensional thinkers sound like cavemen, or cave people to be more politically correct and socially sensitive, but it is a valid question to ask what other dimensions there could be. The answer is that there are endless other dimensions of thinking. So, for anyone who is going to read this chapter and want to say that I left out this or that, I am heading that off at the pass now. I know there are other dimensions of thinking available. There are endless dimensions of thinking. I am just going to discuss some of them in order to stimulate thought on this concept of multi-dimensional thinking.

Some other dimensions of thinking would include Third parties, Unrelated groups, Related groups, Family, External forces that are calculable, External forces that are incalculable, Astrological, Spiritual, Religious, Total logic, Total emotion, Fear, Anger, Greed, Space, Alien, Historical, Psychic, Energetic, Mood, Time, and so forth. It's really endless.

As you can predict by now in reading this book, I am going to offer some examples to illustrate this concept. But first let me define "thinking" as when we have to consider different thoughts in order to come to a decision on something. So for example, the one dimensional view of "self" would be when we are considering what we ourselves need and want, and we do not take anything else into consideration. The two-dimensional thinking of "self" and "the other person" would entail considering what we need and want, and how to get that from the other person, or we are involving that other person into our considerations.

"Third party" dimension would be when we are considering ourselves, the other person directly involved, and also how it would affect yet another third party who might be affected. Let's say I am thinking of moving. I would consider my own wants and needs, but also consider the same of my partner or roommate. I might also consider what my landlord may or may not do with this news. The landlord would be the "third party."

Including the consideration of Astrology into my thoughts obviously means not only thinking of my own wants and needs, the needs of others directly involved, the needs of others indirectly involved, but also whether the Astrology points to this being a good time to move or not. Now I am balancing more balls in the air at the same time while giving this decision some thought.

Considering the "Energetic" or "Energy" into the decision means sensing and feeling what the energy is telling me right now. Yes, this is a bit of a psychic or intuitive dimension, but many people like to use their intuition. Thus, while considering all the other dimensions, you will also try to read, feel, and sense what the current energy or mood of the environment surrounding you suggests you should do. The energy or your intuition might be telling you that it's just not the right time to move even if you want to move. You might not even know exactly why it is not the right time to move. But your intuition is saying it is not. It is one of many dimensions of thought to consider in your decision.

External Forces are something to consider in your contemplations. There are the External Forces we can calculate or predict, such as what this might do to our job, travel consequences, or such, and there are External Forces we can't see right now, such as whether or not we will end up with horrible new neighbors that have ten barking dogs that bark at everything and bark at nothing, all of the time. Thinking in terms of the External Forces dimension is a very important one. It is one thing for us to want to move, and we can calculate the feelings of others, as well as the mood of the day, and many other dimensions and factors, but we MUST consider the external consequences of our potential decision. We must consider all consequences from all angles, of both staying where we are, and moving to a new location, and do this for each possible location.

I want to point out for clarity that the other dimensions of thinking do not always involve people. They often involve moods, feelings, and concrete consequences. The consequences are sometimes predictable, and the consequences are often not predictable. It is a very common mistake for humans to never consider the unpredictable consequences. Remember, it is not the seen enemy that will get you, as much as it is the unseen enemy that will get you. How do you fight an enemy that is unseen? Well, you simply assume they are there even if you can't see them. Consequences are the same way. Whenever I am planning to do something, I always know that something will go wrong, even if I do not know what that will be. Thus, I plan on something going wrong even if I can't tell you what that will be. That is a crucial dimension of thinking, and a great example of how important multi-dimensional thinking becomes.

An important dimension that some people do not understand well is the dimension of Time. Time is the science and art of knowing when to execute your decision. The best laid plans might fail if done at the wrong time. Yet, if you choose the correct time, your plan has a better chance of succeeding. Time is key. But why is this? Does it matter if I do something tomorrow or one month from now? Does it matter if it is done on a Tuesday or a Wednesday? Does it matter if it is done at 10:00AM or 1:00PM? Well, maybe yes and maybe no. I am trying to be a multi-dimensional thinker, so I won't cast judgement on the possibilities, all of which could be valid for strange unknown reasons.

But let me explain why Time itself is multi-dimensional. The dimension of Time may not apply to just whether something should be done now or in a month. It might not be the calendar or clock that is important here. There is another dimension to the dimension of Time. It relates to External Forces. The reason that Time can be a major dimension to consider is that the time you choose to execute your plan might dictate which External Forces you end up facing. The

97

reason why is that External Forces can be very time-dependent. This means that some External Forces won't be a factor during certain time-frames, while other External Forces will be a major factor during other certain time-frames. Thus, Time and External Forces are linked in a multi-dimensional way. With multi-dimensional thinking, you have to consider all the different ways and angles that different things can be related and unrelated. It is a giant multi-dimensional and multi-angle puzzle with moving pieces in multiple dimensions of space and time, as well as other frames of reference.

Another common dimension is to consider your spiritual or religious feelings into your decisions. This is a very personal, but important dimension to consider for many people. Very often this dimension of thinking might conflict with our other dimensions. For example, what I may WANT personally, or what someone else wants, or what gives the least external consequences, may not be in alignment with my spiritual or religious values. We must consider and balance all of our dimensions of thinking even if they conflict.

I also want to mention that there are some negative dimensions that you need to be aware of and remain wary. Fear, Anger, and Greed are three of them. Yes, there are plenty of people who make their mental considerations based upon only one of these dimensions. There are people who make all their decisions from a place of fear. They usually either do nothing, or they will choose the course of action that scares them the least. Making a decision out of fear is always wrong.

Others make decisions while in a state of Anger. Decisions made while angry are always bad decisions. If you are angry, this should be a signal to you that you are not to make any decisions until you calm down. Nothing good can happen while angry. Avoid thinking in this dimension at all costs.

Making decisions based upon Greed will also get you into trouble. Greed is a human temptation that leaves us vulnerable to bad choices that result in bad consequences down the road. The consequences from greed can often be delayed for a very long time, but eventually those consequences will be there to bite you, and will likely be very hungry when they do bite.

Multi-dimensional thinking does not just apply to dimensions of thought for making decisions or considering actions. Multi-dimensional thought is also the opposite of binary thinking. Too many people live in a binary world and think in binary terms. For example, people in a binary world think in terms of good or bad, yes or no, good or bad, right or wrong, smart or stupid, and so forth.

I see binary thinking a lot in arguments. A person will often make a statement of position, and the other person will say, "That is totally wrong," or they may say, "That is wrong and stupid." The person will make snap judgements using binary thought. But that does not mean the person is wrong. HA! I am giving you an example of multi-dimensional thought here. The example being, that even though the person is using archaic binary thought does not mean their conclusion is wrong. In other words, a person can be wrong and right both at the same time. I can call the person stupid if I want, but the person still might come up with the correct conclusion using their stupid method. So, are they really stupid if they come up with the correct conclusion using an archaic flawed method? No, they are not stupid. They are someone who used an old flawed method of thinking to come up with a correct answer. That is me giving a multi-dimensional answer in that previous sentence.

A person can be a well-respected genius, and still make a decision or offer a solution that fails. So at that point, are they smart or stupid? A binary thinker would struggle with this question. They truly would. They would be forced into choosing whether it is more important that the person is a genius, or is it more important that the decision and solution suggested was wrong and failed? A multi-dimensional thinker does not have this predicament. A multi-dimensional thinker would say that the person is really smart, but their solution failed. Put more crudely, one could say, "The respected genius made a stupid decision."

By the way, for extra credit, can anyone suggest how in the world a respected genius can make a stupid decision? I will offer up two possibilities. First, they possibly did not fully consider all the elements of the Hunter Equation (Future Outcome = Intent + Actions + External Forces + Random Luck) into their decision process. If you don't fully consider all the correction Actions and External Forces, you can get into trouble. OR, secondly, I suggest the genius got lazy and did not fully contemplate all of the different dimensions of thinking available to them.

The point is that two conflicting things can be true at the same time. If that statement breaks your brain, then you are likely a binary thinker. You need to work on that. How can you break out of that way of thinking and become more multi-dimensional? One word. Logic.

Logic allows us to think in terms of facts. Binary thinking forces us to make left or right choices, often based upon our own opinions of what is more important, or more wrong, or more right. This would be an emotional and value-based judgement call. However, a multi-dimensional thinker uses logic. "The smart man made a bad decision." That is a statement of logical fact. Yes, it's conflicting, but it is also a true statement of the facts that happened. Learning to accept that conflicting things can both be true at the same time, is a sign that you are a multi-dimensional thinker. As we evolve, humans will have to acquire this skill and become very good at it. Those who do not will be left chiseling in stone, communicating in only yes or no terms based on limited thinking. Not very evolved. We can do better!

CHAPTER TWELVE

Communication

Is Key

Communication is one of life's most important skills, yet humans are not very good at it, and remain unsophisticated with it.

Many of us struggle at communication. Misunderstandings are everyday occurrences, and even can be spotted in almost every conversation witnessed. Why is this? Why do humans struggle so much with communication, and why are there constant misunderstandings?

There are numerous reasons for this. The primary reason is that most people do not communicate to understand. Instead, they communicate to be heard, and receive either validation or something they were seeking. In other words, a person's motive for communicating is very often one-way and somewhat selfish. People usually care more about the other person understanding and acknowledging their own point, than they care about understanding and acknowledging the other person's point. There are frequent times during communication when a person is talking and making their point, but then does not even listen to what the other person is saying in response.

Most humans just talk AT each other, rather than talking WITH each other. It is very often that two separate people are talking at one another, hoping the other person will understand what they said, validate their points as being correct, and then deliver to them whatever they are seeking. People end up talking past each other when both people are desperate to be heard, but neither of them want to listen.

There is always a lot of talking with communication, but often not much listening. When we learn to be a counselor, the most important thing we learn is the art of listening. Instructors actually have to teach everyone how to listen. That is how foreign of a concept it is to most people. People are so used to talking and convincing someone of something, and then not really listening to the other person. Counseling is, or SHOULD BE, about LISTENING to the person, not speaking at them.

Everyone CRAVES to be listened to. Romantic relationships are often chosen and decided based upon which prospects listen the best. People don't care as much about how smart a person is, and they care even less for the person talking for way too long in an effort to try and prove how smart they are. Much more appealing is the person who LISTENS. Then, if you ask the person a question, and the person responds in a very intelligence way, THAT STEALS THE SHOW AND SEALS THE DEAL. But it is mostly about the listening more than how smart the ultimate answer ends up being.

Let me state it clearly. Communication is about listening.

Let's just let that sit there. Therefore, if humans are to become better and more advanced with communication, it means they have to focus on being the best listeners. For our purposes here, communication is not about how well a politician can articulate his or her positions, or how well a lawyer can convince a judge or jury. Yes, that is part of it, and important, but those are SKILLS that are developed for the purpose of certain jobs. What we are talking about here is communication that all humans must master if they want to truly engage and cooperate within the Universe. The communication we are discussing is about a human art form that if done well, can improve a person's life and success rate. An evolved communication ability is a sexy, powerful, and useful trait to have.

If we are to evolve our ability to communicate, let us focus on listening. You are not just listening to the words a person speaks. It is much more than that. You want to listen to the words, the meaning, the feeling, the motivation, the context, the mood, the purpose, and all the emotions involved.

Do not just focus on WHAT they are saying. Focus more on WHY they are saying it. The real meaning behind someone's words is hidden within their motivation for speaking. Remember, communication among humans is mostly selfish and based upon something the person needs or wants. So when a person is speaking, try and listen for what their motivation is. What does this person want? Why are they speaking to you in this way with these words? What is their MOTIVATION?

You might be able to identify their motivation as them trying to convince you of something, get something from you, or them seeking validation that their ideas are correct or of value. Or they are experiencing feelings that they are trying to express so that others understand their pain, such as with venting.

103

We all understand venting. When someone is off on a venting rant, we don't bother to respond to each and every thing the person says. Why? Because the words do not matter. The person is not seeking an answer. The person is actually seeking some emotional relief. Speaking all the words to someone can provide them with emotional relief. This is a great example of when we are not speaking in response, but rather just listening. Listening is what they wanted while they rant and vent.

We see the same thing when someone is crying or upset. Sometimes their words do not even make any sense. Luckily, the words are not the point. The point is to release some mental anguish, and to perhaps allow the other person to UNDERSTAND the emotional grief so that they can later respond in a helpful supportive way. This is when the listener will eventually get a chance to speak, perhaps to give advice when the person is ready to hear it. But first, there is a lot of listening to be done. But listen carefully, because there will be a test later on. When you might have to speak later on with advice, you had better been listening very carefully, so that you can fully understand the person's emotional distress and situation.

Listen to the emotion and feeling. Often people are at a loss for words, do not have a very developed vocabulary, or do not express themselves in words very well. This is why you must listen to the emotion and feeling. There are many moments when I am working with clients, and they express how they do not have the words to explain their feelings to me. My response is that I don't need the words, I just need to understand their FEELINGS. A person can communicate in terms of different feelings and you can fully understand what they are trying to say.

When I am trying to understand what someone wants to communicate, I often try to connect with them on an empathic level. This means I use my own abilities as an Empath to focus on the

104

person and sense their emotions and thoughts. The person does not need to use many words. I just need to sense and feel what the person is feeling. I then match up their feelings with their intended motivation or need. When you match a person's feelings with their motivation, you get communication. It is almost like an equation. So again, figuring out the motivation of why the person is trying to communicate is super important. You want to sense the feelings and emotions behind their thoughts so that you can truly UNDERSTAND what they are intending. Notice I am not speaking much about what words they are saying or how to interpret their words. It's not important. The words are not important at all sometimes. Once you see that, you realize how archaic and unsophisticated most human communication is, since most people only consider the words they say, along with words they might hear in return if they are even listening.

What does this mean for evolution? Humans need to evolve and become more sophisticated with communication. Let us for a moment contemplate the ultimate form of communication. What would be the ultimate form of communication? The answer is, telepathy. With telepathy, people would be able to read each other's mind. So, no words would even be spoken, and all feelings, motivations, needs, emotions, exasperations, and so forth, would be fully "seen" and sensed during the telepathic connection. In an instant, both people would be in full communication that is void of misunderstanding. Telepathy is the most perfect method of communication.

I believe that humans are capable of telepathy, but would need to develop it and practice it. Many humans think telepathy would be amazing and cool, but after they think about it, they would be scared of it. Why? Well, because with telepathy, the other person sees the whole truth. My goodness, can you imagine the other person always seeing the whole truth of your thoughts? YIKES! Imagine your mother-in-law reading your true thoughts! HA! Okay, well some of us adore our mother-in-laws if we have them, but you get my point.

If given the choice, many humans would actually opt out of telepathy for the above reason. Instead, they would prefer to stay with the old archaic incomplete and inaccurate method of verbal communication. This way they can continue to hide their true feelings, true intentions, and can get away with lying. Not very evolved, is it? Well, this is why many humans do not seem to evolve very quickly. Sometimes it's a choice.

With all that said, I believe being skilled and experienced at telepathy would be able to filter what is seen and not seen. Just because you are communicating with telepathy does not mean the other person has access to everything in your mind. They do not. At least in my thinking they would not. My theory is that telepathy would be limited to thoughts, facts, and information, that the person INTENDS to convey. In this way, each person would have control over what information is conveyed telepathically. Like everything else, this would be a skill developed with maturity and practice.

In summary, the most simplistic form of communication is one person talking while not listening. The next level up is when both people talk and listen to each other. The next layer up would be when one or more of the parties are very highly skilled at listening and can understand a tremendous amount by listening to the motivations and feelings behind the communication. The next step up from that would be when one or both parties can empathically connect and understand through very subtle clues, such as emotions, moods, thoughts, and so forth. Then the ultimate form of communication would be a telepathic connection. A person can evolve up through those layers if they put in the effort.

However, I want to discuss other means of communication as well. Let's talk about music. I believe that music is a common language of the Universe. If I were going to try and communicate with alien beings for the first time, I might try music if they did not speak

106

our language, and I was not able to connect telepathically. Music is amazing. Every teenager knows they can fully express their feelings to a person just by sending them a specific song. Music is something that is heard and felt. Love, sadness, pain, joy, excitement, doom, hope, and most any other emotion you can think of, can be expressed through music. It is a universal language.

Additionally, I believe Love is the language of God and the Universe. Again, it is a method of communication and language that other creatures of the Universe would likely relate to. Thus, expressions of caring, compassion, and love go a long way in communicating intentions and feelings. Someone who goes out of their way to communicate with love is likely worth listening to. If a spaceship landed in my backyard, I would likely try to offer a gesture of love, compassion, and caring first. That is most likely to be embraced, or at least accepted as a friendly intention, and not get me zapped by a space blaster.

Everything I am mentioning is only useful if you take the time and effort to evolve yourself and develop these skills and abilities. So, whenever you have a chance, practice your listening skills. Practice understanding through empathy, emotions, and motivations. Build your empathic abilities. A more advanced form of empathic connection will be telepathy. If all else fails, try music and love. Listen to music more carefully for the feelings and meanings it gives you. Open up more and sense more. This is how you become better at communication. By LISTENING.

CHAPTER THIRTEEN

Can't We All Just Get Along?

Why can't we all just get along? Why don't we all just hold hands and sing *Kumbaya*? Surely, we can love each other as brother and sister? Is this where I should say, "We are one," and "Namaste?" What planet would I be living on? Surely not Earth. If I was a worthy spiritual guru, I would be able to smile and say something short and clever that sounds so easy. You might feel better for five minutes and think I am very positive and full of love and light. But we would all be living in a delusion. I thought we pledged to try and not do that in this book (live in a delusion). So alas, I think we need to examine reality. Ugh. Do we have to? Reality is so, well, realistic and not fun. Well, don't worry, we will make our way through this, but we will do it in reality-based way so that maybe what we come up with something practical and useful. We can do this! Have faith!

Let us start with the assumption that some of us will never get along. Some of us WILL get along. Sometimes, many of us might get along. But we will never ALL get along. Prove me wrong if you want. I am sorry if this is a downer for some, or seems pessimistic, but I am not here to only spread glitter and glee. I am here to be truthful and realistic so that we can affect real change, and evolve into better lives. Avoiding problems or pretending they do not exist is not a good way to solve them or make things better. Blindly being optimistic in the face of an obvious problem is really more of a denial approach. It is much healthier and more constructive to sometimes be critical, or even cynical, and face our problems and demons so that we can actually solve them. Evolved humans do not live in false realities, or view problems with false perceptions. Instead, we put on our glasses so we can see clearly, and we start to construct solutions to what we SEE in reality, not what we wish we were seeing in a false reality.

When I talk about us not getting along, I am speaking from two frames of perspectives. First, I am referring to all of us as a society, and secondly, I am referring to our individual personal interactions with friends and family. Those are the two perspectives where all of us could use some help in improving how we approach conflict and deal with people we absolutely do not get along with, and sometimes don't even like.

After we admit that everyone will never get along, and that we will always disagree with people, the next step is for us to identify what our goal is in dealing with such people. I submit to you that the goal should be primarily two items. First is to never get into loud, harsh, out of control emotional arguments and confrontations with people. Doing this is useless and serves no purpose. Once people get upset, they are no longer listening to you anyways, and they certainly are not thinking with reason and logic. Once people have reached a certain point, they are totally committed to their position, no matter how wrong or insane their position may be.

Arguing with anyone at that point is more a matter of venting anger and frustration. It will not result in anyone actually changing their opinions or positions. You will never "win" the argument because nobody is willing to admit defeat. Everyone thinks they are correct, even if they are clearly wrong. I know that is an illogical statement, but humans are illogical creatures. My observations and strategies are often not based upon what is right and wrong, but rather based upon the irrational and illogical psychology of humans. This is why you will often see someone telling a wise old sage he or she is wrong, and the wise sage will often reply, "I know." The wise sage says this because he or she is wise enough to know the argument is a waste of time and energy, and wise enough to know it cannot end until the other person believes they have won or is right. A wise sage knows that saying he or she was wrong does not mean they were wrong. In fact, whenever a wise old sage tells you they are wrong, without any supporting evidence, you should be very suspicious that they just think you are too ignorant for them to argue with you.

I hope I have made a point that arguing is to be avoided, which is one of our primary goals. I also want to point out that rational discussions and debating is not arguing. Anything calm and rational is encouraged. The second primary goal is to establish some kind of common ground with the person whom you are dealing. Searching for and identifying common ground is a very useful skill to learn in not only conflict avoidance and resolution, but also in the art of negotiation.

One of my first lessons in negotiation I actually learned from watching *Star Trek* many years ago. It was an episode where the starship *Enterprise* had to deliver one of the galaxy's greatest negotiators to an important meeting where he was going to mediate a peace between two species or races of beings who had been at war for centuries. Someone asked the negotiator how he was going to get these two groups to agree to a peace. I can't remember all the details, but he said the most important step had already been achieved, which was to get BOTH parties to WANT a peaceful agreement. The actual desire of both parties to want to reach an agreement is very powerful. If one group does not care to reach any agreement, there is very little hope. But both parties wanting an agreement raises the chances for success greatly.

Once you have both parties wanting to agree, the next step he said, was to find one shred of something, anything, that both of them have in common and can agree on. The negotiator mentioned that the two parties had argued for months just about what shape the negotiating table they sit at should be. If they could not even agree on the shape of a table, then what hope would there be of a peace agreement? Well, the answer, and the magic of the negotiator, was to somehow find ONE THING that both parties had in common and could agree on, no matter how small or insignificant it might seem.

And yes, most everything I needed to know in life, I learned from *Star Trek*. Okay, joking, but maybe not joking. My point is that this concept made a big impression on my young impressionable mind at the time. I realized it had truth to it, and was perhaps the secret to handling most conflicts. I still believe this today.

Thus, one of your primary goals in dealing with anyone you absolutely do not get along with or agree with, should be to desperately find and figure out some common ground you might share with this person. I view common ground and a shared point of agreement as the same thing. An example might be if you both agree it is way too hot out today. That is a matter of commonality and something you both agree on.

Let's run through an example. Let us say you are in some kind of a setting where you are stuck dealing with a family member, work associate, or someone else who you absolutely do not get along with or agree with. Let's pretend they are spouting off about politics or something else, and you think they are totally insane, ignorant, naïve, stupid, crazy, and even offensive. Your first instinct will be to become upset listening to their nonsense. They are pushing all kinds of buttons and you are dying to tell them how stupid they are. If you want to take the evolved approach, you will push the pause button in your head and first realize one thing.

You will realize and remember that arguing with such a person is useless, pointless, and will have no productive outcome. Thus, logically, arguing with them would be a waste of time and resources. You are evolved and think more logically now. You will not engage in things that serve no purpose, and even worse, might create a problem or conflict you did not have before.

You will then remember your goals in dealing with such people you don't get along with, or don't like. You will remember rule number one, which is to never argue when it will get nasty, heated, and will serve no practical purpose. Thus, at this point you have your "calm button" on.

In order to shut this person up and de-escalate the rising temperatures, you remember that the next course of action is for you to find some item of commonality or agreement between you and this other person.

Search everywhere and search fast. Observe if they are wearing something you like. Observe if they arrived in a vehicle you like. Remember if they have said anything about their work, family life, life background, or even places they have traveled. Have a very open mind and make it process information like a fast super computer. FIND SOMETHING. If you get stuck, look around your immediate environment at the weather conditions, trees, birds, scenery, or anything. Find something to comment on. Hopefully, make your comment relevant to something this person has mentioned or you noticed about them. You can even ask them if they have "been here before." Maybe it is both of your first times being at this location at this gathering. That is commonality. Maybe you both have the same beverage and you are both enjoying it. That is commonality and agreement.

However small, find that one item of commonality and agreement. It's there somewhere. That will change the subject, de-escalate the discussion, and put you both in a better place of commonality and agreement. After a while, hopefully you can accidentally stumble upon a more substantial item of commonality. For example, maybe you both recently lost a loved one or pet, or you both have the same breed of dog or cat. If you can find a substantial item of commonality such as this, you can then have a more genuine discussion about something you both have in common on a more human level. Having such a discussion will make you see that even though you disagree with this person on most everything, you ARE still able to relate to them in some substantial way. There is magic in this. When both people can relate to each other on a very human, emotional, deep level, their guard starts to come down, and two people can begin to see each other differently. With time, this can develop into a very positive, even if limited, friendship. You both might agree to not discuss politics or whatever you disagree on, but you both realize that you share some things that are worth discussing and interacting. THIS type of interacting is exactly what we need more of in this world.

We need to stop screaming at each other about things we will never agree on. Instead, we need to find those genuine human items we share in common that we can relate with each other on in a sincere way.

This concept applies to anyone you meet in society, but also applies to your family relationships. Many people dread family holidays

113

because they know the disagreements and arguments are coming. We need to learn to limit the direction of our discussions, and use the skills we are discussing to steer interactions in a more friendly enjoyable direction.

An evolved person knows how to navigate a nasty unproductive conversation into one of commonality and agreement. Once we learn how to agree on at least one thing, we can build from that. Once humans learn to build from a foundation of one item of agreement, society will evolve into something better and more productive so that we all may live better lives. An evolved world will need to unite us as a people even when we disagree.

CHAPTER FOURTEEN

Relationships

If we evolve from within first, and then this causes things to evolve outwardly, like a ripple from a stone being thrown into a pond, we would then be remiss if we did not examine how our relationships might evolve.

Our current relationships usually mirror our inner self. If inside we are toxic, then our relationship will be toxic. If inside we are abused, then our relationship may be abusive. If inside we are limited, then our relationship will be limited. If inside we do not feel worthy, then our relationship will likely not be worthy. This is not The Law of Attraction. This is called human psychology. You can't just flip the script by thinking a happy thought instead of a negative one. You cannot just "decide" to be worthy. What you must do is RECONDITION YOUR MIND, as a way of healing from traumas that have damaged or inhibited your psyche and psychological behavior from healthier and happier states of mind and relationships.

It's hard work. It requires a lot of self-work: "shadow work" as they say, facing your demons head-on, and doing all of this over a good period of time. It sounds like I am talking about fixing your inner-self rather than evolving. That is true. If you have gotten this far through the book, then you have realized that the first things we focused on were things that were broken and needed to be fixed. But now, we are continuing to reach forward toward unrealized potential and future possibilities, within ourselves and the world.

Thus, this chapter had to first acknowledge that when it comes to relationships, you must first fix what is broken before you expect to evolve forward. Here is how I see it. I imagine three states of relationships. First, is a broken relationship. Second is a healthy relationship. The third is an evolved relationship. The first is obvious, but I wanted to make a point that there is a stark difference between the second two.

A healthy relationship in today's terms tends to be one where both people are getting along well together. There are likely traditional ROLES that each person is playing within the relationship. It does not matter whether the relationship is straight, or gay, or what have you. There are certain roles that each person tends to take on, such as a dominant or submissive position in the relationship. A healthy relationship tends to divide up these roles so that each person is dominant in some roles, but submissive in others. A relationship where one person is dominant in all roles, and the other submissive in all roles, tends to be more unhealthy, although there are always exceptions. Today's healthy relationships normally consists of expectations and a platform of values and ideas, much like a political party. Both people sign onto this general basic platform. If everything goes well, as expected, and nothing much changes, the relationship tends to go well.

There is a major vulnerability and weakness within this structure of today's healthy relationship. It can be summed up in one word. Change. I know that word is very familiar to you by now. Everything changes. Everyone changes. Nothing lasts forever. In discussing healthy relationships of today, I made a point of saying that everything goes well as long as nothing unexpected happens, or nothing much changes. That statement alone, is a statement of false thinking. You get bonus points if you caught that. It is false thinking because obviously things will not go as planned, and obviously things will change. Thus, we can expect most healthy relationships to run into trouble.

These days, many people do not even want to get married. It is a terrifying prospect due to the daunting failure rate. Those who do get married very often get divorced. I might even be so bold to say that MOST who get married get divorced. If that is bad enough, the few remaining who don't get a divorce, are often remaining in miserable marriages. That only leaves us a tiny fraction of relationships that remain intact and happy. If I wanted to be cynical, I might say that those in relationships that didn't get married, might be doing a little better, but usually not. Breakups are all around us like leaves falling off the trees in Autumn during a wind storm.

Frankly, why would anyone even want to attempt a relationship anymore with eventual failure being almost certain? Well, there are some reasons. First of all, hope springs eternal. You never know, things might work out great for you. However, humans are terrible at math and statistics. Humans think with their emotional brain instead of their logical brain. If a human is told that something has a 5% success rate, nearly all humans will assume they can be, and will be, part of that 5%. If it wasn't so sad, it would be comical. But enough of my "Negative Nancy" gloom-and-doom-sour-grapes-attitude. My apologies to everyone named Nancy. I don't mean anything by it.

Let's look at the more serious reasons for attempting a

relationship. Most humans prefer companionship rather than being alone. Humans usually do not do well alone in isolation. Humans want and need companionship on some level. Another reason is more practical. It is simply easier to survive in life if you have a partner. Two people earning money for life's expenses can make life so much easier and better. Couples learn this after divorce when both have to lower their standard of living from what they enjoyed together. So yes, the reason is financial in a nutshell. A third major reason is for sexual companionship. Humans tend to be sexual creatures and want regular safe access to sex with someone they trust and are comfortable with.

So, what do we have so far? The reasons for attempting a relationship are for companionship (so we are not alone), financial (so we can afford to survive), and for sex (because well, because). Are there any others? Of course there are. There is also something called love. Yes, I understand that some people believe they have a better chance of finding Sasquatch walking down Main Street carrying a stuffed unicorn doll, than they have of finding love. I get it. But alas, here we come full circle to the whole "hope springs eternal" thing. You never know. You could find true love, and plenty of people do.

However, when it comes to love, there are many different types of love. There is something we will call "initial relationship love." This often manifests as "love at first sight." This is when you see that person and something clicks inside you. They are at the perfect frequency, you "feel" them even though you do not know them, and you are super attracted. You get to know them and everything is perfect. They have similar values and goals to you, and their routines seem compatible with yours. You gaze into each other's eyes and kiss under the moonlight on a perfect summer night. You never break eye contact as the kiss turns into a sexual encounter that feels so intense that you pray all your parts and pieces remained where they were supposed to be afterwards, because it was as if all of the sexual energy and tension had exploded into universal space. After sex, they don't run off, and you become even more attached than before the sex. You are in love. They are your "forever person." I wanted to add a line in here about them riding in on a unicorn, but my editor said no. However, as perfect as this picture is, and as intensely as your toes curled during the encounter, we are talking about a moment in time. This is the "honeymoon phase," or as I said, "initial relationship love." Eventually, real life pushes its foot back in the door like a drunken brute back from a long stay at a bar on a bender. Some event in one of your lives might happen that change the dynamics and tests the relationship.

Initial relationship love is very delicate and fragile. It exists in a bubble where the difficult facts, circumstances, external forces, and old baggage of life, do not exist. It is easier to fall in love, and love someone, when all the things I just mentioned have not yet reared their ugly head. Once one or more of those items poke their head through the bedroom door, the new love can be tested. It SHOULD be tested. This is when the beautiful initial love we all crave and dream of, starts to fade and transfers into a more substantial love, OR the relationship starts to die off. Which usually happens to you? You don't need to answer that.

What on Earth am I even babbling about? Well, I am trying to show why relationships need to evolve. They need to evolve from the "initial first love" to a "substantial lasting love." But even the "substantial "lasting love needs to evolve, because we already discussed what happened to most established relationships and marriages.

So how do we do this? How are relationships going to evolve? And why did I not just start this chapter with this key question and paragraph? Why did I force you to endure all the previous babblings first? All good questions. Firstly, we never hand out candy without earning it first. We have to understand the pain and the problem before we can truly appreciate the solution. I hope I have clearly outlined how the current relationship prototypes could use some improvement, even if you happen to be in a fairly healthy and happy relationship presently.

For me, my view of an evolved relationship would be a mirror image of you as an evolved person. We have had discussions about more advanced and healthy thinking. There is a sense of empowerment, clarity, and strength in the more evolved person you are becoming. There is a notion of thinking in multiple dimensions. We discussed thinking in a very independent way, as well as having advanced communication skills. We went over numerous human frailties that need to be checked upon and repaired. Most importantly, we embraced the idea of CHANGE as being necessary, good, and a reality. So, having taken all of those enhancements in mind for your inner-self, I would expect your relationships to evolve in a similar way.

This means your relationship should not be a mirror image of something that is broken within you. Instead, your relationship should be a mirror image of the strength, wisdom, and empowerment within you. This would only be as a result from your very hard work in improving and healing yourself. You want to do the most healing and self-work you possibility can so that it will reflect within your relationship. The better you are, healthier you are, more empowered you are, the more your relationship will reflect all of those things.

Furthermore, I do not expect to see as many fixed traditional roles in evolved relationships. Evolved humans will begin to be more equal to each other in their capabilities and potential. Therefore, there is no need for fixed traditional roles. I believe evolved relationships will have more of a cooperative nature to them, rather than competition for power in certain roles. And yes, there really are couples that compete with each other on different levels. It becomes unhealthy and toxic.

I almost don't have to describe an evolved relationship, because it will be everything you already read about involving evolved individuals. You can imagine how you want to evolve, and that will be how your evolved relationship will look. Change starts within you, then it can transfer to your relationships, after which it can transfer to society as a whole.

But what about love? What about curling toes? Do we get to keep that? Well yeah, why wouldn't we? Evolving does not mean giving up the fun and excitement of the old ways. Evolving only means being more advanced, sophisticated, and more mature than the old ways.

I think an evolved relationship will mean having the initial honeymoon phase, but with the full knowledge that we need to be examining below the surface and trying to find building blocks of a substantial lasting love. What does this mean? I think a substantial and lasting love is built upon the premise that two people want to enter into a partnership that will each make them both a better person because they are together. The old corny phrase of "You make me a better person" is not old and corny. It is evolved, but of course I would say "We make each other better people by being together."

The phrase of "You complete me" is not evolved. It is old and corny. An evolved person does not need anyone to complete them. An evolved person completes themselves, thank you very much. So it's not about that. It is about two people feeling better together, living better together, and reaching higher levels of potential together. It is a symbiotic cooperative union where the whole is much greater than the two separately.

All of what I said above still exists at the same time as each person also still maintains a self-empowerment of independence. Nobody owns the other person, and the two people do not own each other. Each person keeps their own power. The evolution is that each person is mature enough to keep their power, respect the other person's own power, and still are able to work together for a greater outcome.

Respect is key. The two respect each other for their contributions, attributes, and abilities. If there is no respect, forget it and walk away. Don't waste your time. Mutual respect is mutual love. There is no love without respect. If they do not respect you, they do not love you. They are only using you. Do not be afraid to see the truth. An evolved person does not live in delusion and false thinking. An evolved person faces the facts, and makes sound choices of change when needed.

I have saved the most important factor for last. Change. That word again! An evolved relationship EXPECTS change, knows it is coming, accepts it, and even embraces it. This is the most difficult part of any relationship. It is easy to maintain a relationship when you are comfortable with all the established circumstances and routines. But what happens when there are major changes? Well, most often it's breakup time. This is where the real evolution must take place.

Do not enter into a relationship without accepting that change is coming. Expect both the circumstances, and other person, to change. You will change as well. Fully accept, expect, and explore this before you even commit. Communicate with your partner about this issue. You must both have a deep understanding of what change can do to a relationship. Realize that unexpected twists and turns are coming. Talk to each other about how you might handle that when it comes. Talk about WHY you are together.

Are you only together because the Sunday pancakes are really good? Are you together because you can afford that nice home you wanted? OR, are you together because you want to help each other become better people, and you know that IN THE END, you will both end up in a better place together than if you tried to get there separately? All of the hard questions and issues should be discussed before commitment.

An evolved relationship will be well built and braced for changes to come. THAT is what will make it evolved. The love is the same, the toe curling is the same, the convenient financial arrangement is the same. What is different is the concept of expecting, accepting, and embracing change. If a relationship can deal with change effectively, and advantageously, then it will indeed be evolved beyond what we usually see today.

CHAPTER FIFTEEN

When People Think Your Dreams Are Stupid

How many of us are sick and tired of others thinking or even saying that our hopes and dreams are stupid? Or irresponsible? Or unrealistic? It is like they think we are stupid for having the dreams we have. Their criticism makes it obvious, but also the looks, mannerisms, and energy they exude is enough to put a damper on our struggle to maintain our enthusiasm for finding any happiness or hope in our lives.

Do you know what dreams are? Dreams are MAGIC. Our dreams

are the one way we can keep magic and hope in our lives. As long as we have dreams, anything can happen. If anything can happen, we have hope. Having hope is the fuel for fighting and beating depression. Hope is life.

We are all different. Different is beautiful. If everyone was the same, thought the same things, and had the same dreams, our world would be boring. Do you know where inspiration comes from? Inspiration comes from seeing or watching what another person is doing, or has done, that we didn't think was possible for us do. The inspirational thought is, "Hey if they can do that, then maybe I can also." This would never happen if people with different ideas and thinking did not ACT upon their ideas and dreams. Because they took the leap and did something about THEIR dreams, we now dare to dream that we can do something similar.

Inspiration, dreams, and hope are all the nectar of life. Without them, one would have to ask why we are here, and how we are existing in our struggles. If we don't see inspiration, have dreams, or feel much hope, are we really living? The lack of the aforementioned items can lead to not only depression, but suicidal thoughts. So, when I say inspiration, dreams, and hope, IS LIFE, I am being literal.

In my book *Heal Me*, I discuss suicide in more detail. My "suicide equation" is: Incredible Pain + Hopelessness = Suicide. When helping those with suicidal thoughts, we are left with that equation to deal with. The goal is to decrease the level of pain, or decrease the level of hopelessness. If you can do one or both of those things, you can rescue yourself or someone else from potential suicide. A major component or ingredient of hope is having dreams. A dream is that magical spark of light that powers hope. If we can dream, we will have hope.

If having dreams are this critical to a person's happiness and very survival, why then is there a tendency for society and those around us to bash, criticize, and discourage our dreams? The answer lies within their humanity and psychology.

Remember, most of the time we are dealing with humans that are fairly unevolved. Humans tend to view life from one dimension and perspective, that being their own dimension of "self." Most people will view and judge your dreams from their own perspective and experiences only. There tends to be two types of people who attack your dreams. The first are people who are simply trying to drag you down to their level, and the second are people who are "concerned," but their concern is doing more harm than good.

First, let us discuss the first group of trolls who just want to keep you down on their level, and really don't even care what your dreams are. They may be jealous that you have a dream that inspires you, and is uplifting you to a level much higher than the misery they themselves are living within. These are people that are desperately trying to find ways to make themselves feel better, and a popular way for these folks to feel better about themselves is to see other people as miserable, or more miserable, than they are.

These folks will dismiss your dreams out-of-hand without even fully listening and understanding them. Most of these people are not acting only out of evilness or to be mean. These people are actually suffering and deserve compassion on a human level, although deserve none of your thought on an intellectual level. These people have likely had some hard breaks and have had their own dreams crushed in the past. A lot of us actually know what this feels like. So, don't think that I am trashing this group of people. Me and others can relate to this group of people in terms of the failures, disappointments, frustration, and anger they feel from their own past experiences. The difference between us and them is that instead of tearing others down to comfort ourselves, we try to teach and uplift others who can learn from our experiences. Right? Yes, that's right.

However, many others will see your dreams only through their own perspective and single dimensional thinking. That is, they see dreams as being impossible, and subject to inevitable failure. Seeing or hearing you talk about your dreams reminds them of the inspiration and hope they once had themselves. That triggers within them very traumatic and hurtful memories and feelings. They respond to this triggering by lashing out. Their first instinct is to put you back down to reality, and show you the failure and pain they feel from their own past experiences.

Obviously, this reaction is not even logical. Their past experiences with their own dreams have no bearing on the outcome of your dreams. But they are human, so thus they are thinking out of emotion and hurt instead of logic. Their own perspective is that dreams are for fools, because that is how THEY feel. They feel foolish for once believing in their dreams, only to have them fail miserably. Again, I have great sympathy for these people because I have had plenty of my own destroyed dreams and miserable failures. But I realize that my experiences in life do not dictate other people's experiences in life.

So, when you face this type of dream basher, you should immediately realize that they are only seeing your dreams from their own perspective, and not from the perspective of reality and possibility. Furthermore, they are only expressing their own pain by taking the position they are taking against your dreams. They are engaging in a normal human instinct of tearing you down so that they are not the only ones feeling miserable. Realizing all of this does not make it less annoying, but it should make it less significant, such that it is not important or relevant to you.

The second group of people who attempt to burn down your dreams are those who are actually concerned for your outcomes and well-being. These people are very often parents, family, friends, or life partners. This group is certainly not intentionally trying to hurt you. They ACTUALLY THINK they are being helpful and saving you from harm. But alas, they are making the same mistake as the first group. They are only viewing your dreams through their own perspectives with a one-dimensional view.

This group is very risk-averse, meaning they do not want to see you take risks that might result in a negative or harmful outcome to you. They might be thinking, "That seems difficult and unlikely, so you should not consider it." They might be drawing upon their own past experiences of failure regarding taking risks for their own failed dreams.

This group is not trying to drag you down to their level of misery. Rather, this group is trying to make you more careful in taking risks. This group does not want to see you suffer any negative consequences from you following your dreams. To them, it is better to discourage you from following your dreams, than to see you chase your dreams and suffer a painful failure. However, this group is very misguided and short-sighted.

This group does not realize that the loss of your dreams, or lack of any dreams, is far worse than chasing dreams that do not work out. This is the group that will tear down your dreams, leave you with no inspiration or hope to live for, watch you fall into depression, suicidal thoughts, and their response will be to show you sympathy for your misery, but never realize that they actually had a role in this devastating outcome by tearing down your dreams.

Let me restate the above concept more clearly because it is so important. The ability to chase and follow your dreams is much more important than sparing yourself from potential failure by not following your dreams at all.

There are a lot of parents reading this right now who are probably questioning my advice on this issue. They have valid concerns for their child's success, mental well-being, and them having a successful outcome in life. Thus, these are the parents who are crushing dreams that they think are irresponsible, unrealistic, or stupid. I will respectfully disagree with your approach.

I would instead suggest the following regarding a dream that you truly disagree with and think won't end well. I would absorb and digest my point about dreams themselves being more important than the outcome. Then, I would approach the situation with your child differently. First, I would applaud them for having their dream. Tell them anything can happen if they have a dream, work hard, and things work in their favor. Tell them chasing dreams are always a risk because sometimes we fail even though we are sure we won't when we first start out. But tell them that life is about following your dreams and learning along the way from your mistakes, failures, and successes. Next, you can give them your honest opinion of what you think might happen regarding their specific dream. Give supporting details of why you feel this way (facts and evidence, not opinions). But then tell them that if they decide to proceed anyway, you will support them 100% and want nothing more than for them to succeed. Silently, if they fail, you will be there for them to help pick up the pieces, give support, and help them back onto the horse.

Obviously, my approach also applies to friends or other family members, and not just your children. Please do not be a dream destroyer. Be a constructive support for anyone following their dreams. It is much better to let them try and let them fail, than to crush them down before they can even try. If you do that, they may eventually just give up on life and not try anything at all anymore. Let them try. Let them fail. Then help them back up off the ground. The consequences they experience will be invaluable lessons to them so that they will be smarter the next time around. A wise person is one who fails many times and learns, rather than a person who does not try at all and learns nothing.

Now, let me speak to you about following your dreams when you have your own worries about the risks and possible consequences. First, please DO plenty of research, thinking, and planning. I am not suggesting that everyone chase any dream that crosses their mind. I support a person doing a lot of consideration and examining hard facts before taking a risk. The consequences are no joke and I know how serious they can be from my own personal experience.

I recommend at least considering my life equation, the Hunter Equation, when examining possible opportunities or courses of action. As a reminder, the Hunter Equation states: Your Future Outcome = (Intent + Actions + External Forces + Random Luck). This is a useful equation and exercise to put yourself through because it forces you to clearly identify all the action steps you must take to accomplish your goal. It also forces you to consider all of the possible outside External Forces that might impact your success. Doing this gives you a chance to anticipate potential outside problems, and put into place mitigating factors to increase your chances of success. A well thought-out plan is critical, as is the knowledge that your plan absolutely will NOT go as planned. Accept it, anticipate it, and embrace it. Be ready to adjust accordingly.

Assuming you have a dream you believe in, and a plan that is well thought-out and considered, then I beg you to follow your dreams. Chase them to the ends of the Earth until you no longer wish to dream them. As long as you BELIEVE, and as long as your action plan CAN succeed, don't give up. Pursue it until you succeed, or no longer want to pursue that dream. A person is allowed to change their mind. But do not let anyone change your mind for you, and if YOUR mind is not changed about your dream, then never stop chasing it.

Your dreams are your magic. Never let the magic die. Believe in yourself and your dreams. Do not let people who think you are foolish or stupid stop you. It is not their life. They can live their own miserable life. You need to live YOUR life so that it has MEANING TO YOU. Nobody else gets to decide what that is except you.

So when you are feeling down, but still have a dream, well, jump in the car, drive till you meet the sea, then jump onto your sailboat and sail free on the high seas until you are ready to take the leap and fly away free. Fly away with your dreams and see what happens. Whatever the outcome, you will be living your dream, living your truth, and thus living an evolved meaningful life.

CHAPTER SIXTEEN

Competition
Or Cooperation

I wanted to start covering some concepts that might seem general or futuristic in a societal way, but are actually relevant to how we evolve within ourselves. In general, people are usually a reflection of society. If society is cut-throat, devious, or cynical, then people usually mirror that as a way of fitting in and functioning within that society. Obviously, there are lots of exceptions to this rule, and some people specialize and pride themselves at being the opposite of society. But my point is that "the masses" tend to become what surrounds them. We sort of already talked about this societal and mental conditioning in past chapters. Humans will condition themselves and adapt their behavior so that they will be accepted

132

within their given community.

Sometimes we realize that society may not be what we wish it would be, or we as people are not how we wish to be. We desire CHANGE in these circumstances. Now, there is a word that should be familiar to you by now, right? We wish society would change, but we don't control society. However, we do control ourselves. So, if we wish to change ourselves, we can certainly do that. There is a bonus also though. When we change ourselves, we are also contributing to a change in society. Society changes one person at a time. Enough of the masses have to change and align to a new paradigm, AND THEN the leadership must change to recognize the changes within the masses. After that point, society then changes. There are also plenty of arguments to indicate that the leaders may or may not need to change depending on if society changes or not. We will not get into that argument since this particular book is more about the inner being than the outer shell.

What I am trying to get at is that the evolution of society starts with the evolution of the person. Regardless of what you think of society, the real focus should always be on yourself. I do not mean that in a selfish way. I say that because societal change can only come when people change FIRST. This journey we are on is about evolving. It is time to realize that by evolving ourselves from within, we can also cause society and the world to evolve.

I wanted to cover a concept that is relevant to society as a whole, as well as your own interpersonal relationships, career aspirations, and relationships. It is this philosophy of competition vs. cooperation. I promise this is not just a philosophical discussion. I have included it because it can have a direct bearing on how you can advance your position in life by understanding and engaging in an evolved philosophy.

Currently, our general societal philosophy of operation is one of competition. There is this idea that if we want anything in life, we must compete against others and defeat them. "To the winner go the spoils." We must be better, faster, stronger, smarter, and most importantly, we must be more effective at "playing the game" than they are. We must win at any cost by any means.

The competition starts when we are children in school, and Johnny gets a 94 on a test while Timmy gets an 82. We automatically assume that Johnny will get all the good things in life, and Timmy might not. We won't even discuss Derek who got a 62, even though Derek is far more funny and interesting than both Johnny and Timmy.

This competition continues our entire lives. Everyone always has to figure out how to derail you, so that they can get more for themselves. There is a thinking that if I want something, I have to take it from someone else. If I want a certain job, that means someone else has to lose that job. If I want to make the sale, then someone else has to lose the sale. For every winner, there must be a loser is the philosophy.

This philosophy has resulted in a society, and personal lives, that revolve around someone always trying to stab us in the back, while we need to stab others in the back if we are to "win" at "the game." This results in a huge consumption of a person's resources and energy being used to "fight in the game," rather than manifesting a real accomplishment or abundant result. Rather than focusing wholly on creating the best product, idea, or service, we are spending much of our time playing defense against those trying to take us down, and likewise we are having to look for opportunities to take from others so that we might have more.

Remember, this type of "business philosophy" also applies to personal relationships and how people conduct themselves personally. There are always instances of catty dramas with people swiping at each other, so that one person might look better than the other. There is a competition for friends and popularity as if it were a business venture. It is a painful existence that eats up a lot of unnecessary resources and energy. It slows all of us down so that we progress much more slowly, and reach smaller levels of success.

When will we evolve to something better? If we so choose and decide, we can evolve to a higher-level philosophy that gives better results with less resources and energy spent. You see, this is not some naïve discussion on an impossible utopia. This is a relevant discussion that can make businesses more money, as well as enriching each person involved. Everyone, including society as a whole could benefit. It is an economic consideration as much as a societal and personal one.

I am talking about the philosophy of Cooperation, instead of Competition. The idea behind cooperation is that we can reach better results together at a lower cost, than if we competed. This is as much about math as anything else, so I will give an example of the math. Let's say we have two equations, A and B.

A states: Product cost = Material + Labor + Cost of fighting with competitors to steal business and prevent them from stealing ours.

B states: Product cost = Material + Labor

Which equation do you think results in a lower product cost? You know the answer, since equation B does not include the cost of fighting competitors. But the costs can be lowered even more if we combine efforts with a pool of diverse talent.

In a "competitive society", we would have five factories with five different owners, all hoping to get a bigger piece of the pie and make more money than the next guy. Each of the five factories have to build huge expensive facilities and compete for a wide range of talent.

In a "cooperation society", we would still have five different owners wanting to own a factory, but they would work together, doing what each one is strongest at. One of them might have the best facility and so that would be expanded and production consolidated at the better facility. Another one of the businesses might have the best production staff. A different business might have a better office management staff. Another business might have the better sales team. If instead of competing and spending all their energy fighting each other, they combined forces and each offered the best they had to give, then the end-product would be much better, under more efficient management, better quality, and a more effective sales relationship with customers. As a whole, they would sell much more product because of the higher quality and better management. The profit would be much higher without the losses of the competitive fighting.

Now I know some might be thinking that I am suggesting a huge consolidation that results in lack of "market competition." I am not. I am more suggesting separate groups of businesses work together as a whole. This is already being done on a smaller scale in some sectors. Plenty of businesses use outside or independent contractors to perform some duties within their business. I am suggesting more of this. Less of an employee/slave labor theme, and more of an individual independent contractor theme, where the contractors are both individuals, but also large companies. I realize this over-simplification leaves this discussion open to many issues, such as economic, political, and technical. I want to just stick with the general philosophical idea for this book.

I want to bring this back to an individual evolution discussion. I gave the example above, not to start a debate on political economic corporate policy, but rather to inspire a new way of thinking for how each individual operates personally. Instead of looking at a person and thinking, "How can I compete against, and defeat this person," you would instead look at a person and think, "How can I work with this person so that we both have more than we would have if we worked against each separately." That last statement is the point of this whole rambling chapter, and my apologies. But I think each individual on this planet should think of themselves as a valued "self-business" with talent and potential. I think we need to move away from the "mass slave labor" concept.

The "masses" currently think of themselves as a powerless slave who must compete and beat the next person beside them or they will fail. An EVOLVED view would be that we are each valued individuals with unique and special talents, that when combined with others, can created more and better for all, including ourselves.

I am hoping people can bring this thinking down to a very personal level. Let us say you have a goal of achieving something, or creating something. Instead of figuring out how you will compete with others to reach your goal, consider WHO you might be able to work with to achieve it or create it more quickly, efficiently, with less cost, and with a greater quality outcome. Who has talents that compliment yours? I am not suggesting you team up with others who have the exact same talents and ability as you. I am suggesting you team up with others who are different than you, and have different talents and abilities than you.

DIVERSITY is an amazing core strength. I know our society questions diversity in different ways. But a diverse pool of talents, abilities, perspectives, and ideas, make for a powerhouse of potential to produce more and better with less resources. This applies on a business level as well as on a personal level.

I believe an evolved society will stop thinking about how to compete effectively, and will instead think about how they can find more partners of cooperation. People will realize that it's cheaper, easier, and better this way. People no longer need to fight and steal from each other. People can instead focus on complimenting each other so that each person actually gets a much greater reward together than if they kept trying to fight for themselves against everyone else.

For me it comes down to a simple concept I learned as a kid. Let's say you and I are standing in a parking lot full of ice and snow. We are being paid to clear it. We have two choices on how to proceed. First method is that we can both start at opposite ends and meet in the middle. We can see who is faster and gets to the middle sooner, and the fight over who should be paid more. OR, we can see how we might do the job faster by cooperating. Perhaps I suggest that I am a bit better at chopping ice than you, and you seem to be better at pushing the shovel to move it out. Therefore, I might suggest I do the ice chopping and you do the shoveling. We will start in a corner together and work to the other side together. Through this cooperation of using each of our stronger talents together, we would clear the entire parking lot faster. We will have collected our pay and spent less time and resources earning that pay because we leveraged our cooperative talents.

This is how we should be approaching life. How can you and I work together more efficiently so that we both gain a larger benefit? It will not be through competition. It will be through some sort of cooperation. Finally, what do you think will happen to society if enough people start thinking and working like you and I just did in the parking lot? Yes, society will evolve, just like you and I did.

CHAPTER SEVENTEEN

Values

I do not want anyone to get too nervous about the chapter title. I am not about to lecture you or push my values onto you. This chapter is not about any specific values that I feel evolved humans "must" have. This book is NOT about indoctrinating people into any specific political, religious, or spiritual philosophy. In fact, you can give me an elbow if I get too close. I am not trying to dictate values, change your beliefs, or force anything upon anyone. If anything, I have been promoting independent thought and choice. My hope is that people, whoever they are and whatever their beliefs and values, will simply use some of the concepts in this book to EVOLVE beyond what they already are, or who they want to be. I am not trying to dictate who you should become, or judge what is better or worse. I am just trying to do what I do for all my clients, and that is take whatever and whoever you are, and make you even better. I will leave any changes up to you. Consider my concepts as only suggestions for evolving, if you so choose. With that long and repetitive disclosure firmly in place, let us proceed.

This chapter is really an extension of the previous chapter regarding competition vs. cooperation. I wanted to examine two different values systems, one being our present system, and then a more evolved future system. This chapter is about the societal value systems of Greed vs. Love. It might seem clichéd or simple, but there is more to it, and in order to evolve, we must give it some contemplation.

Our current societal values system is based upon Greed, with a capital G. If you feel I say it like that's a bad thing, I don't mean to. I am trying to be very matter-of-fact in this particular discussion. Humans have certain behaviors that come naturally to them, and greed is one of them. I am not judging, but greed is not that pretty. However, it IS quite an effective motivating tool that seems to inspire people to do things they would not normally want to do.

If we pretend greed is a pig (my apologies to pigs), and we want to try and put some pretty lipstick on this pig and make her stunning, then we would describe greed is a natural human compulsion that incentivizes humans to work really hard and acquire all resources (and then some) that they will be needing. I will give this pig a little eyeliner and provide a pretty example of greed.

A squirrel before winter can get very greedy, and will grab, gather, and hoard, as many nuts as he possibly can. The squirrel does not do this because he is an evil master of the animal kingdom. The squirrel is not trying to have total disregard for his fellow squirrel community. The squirrel is doing this in order to ensure survival through a long winter. The squirrel is being greedy and taking more than he can use, in case there is some kind of problem resulting in him needing more nuts than anticipated. Is that bad, or is it smart? One thing for sure, it is animal nature, just like it is human nature.

So, if it's okay for the squirrel to gather as much as possible, including much more than he will ever need, the why is it not okay for humans to be greedy and take more than they need and hoard the extra? Why are humans judged for being greedy and squirrels are not?

The answer is that squirrels have very few options, and humans have many options. A squirrel cannot run down to the Super Stop Grocery Store and pick up some nuts in aisle 9. However, humans can. There is another difference between squirrels and humans. Squirrels have not developed a large organized world-wide civilization that humans have. Most of the world's greatest philosophers have been humans and not squirrels. That is not to say that squirrels won't someday produce better philosophers. The way things are heading, I would say it's likely they may. When they do, I hope we humans take notice and listen to what the great squirrel has to say.

Silliness aside, humans are guilty of greed, and squirrels are not. Humans are greedy because it's a natural compulsion they choose to live by, and choose to not evolve beyond it. Why evolve from greed some might ask? If greed is a natural human compulsion, and it provides a natural incentive to work hard and acquire things, then why not just leave it alone and let it thrive?

The answer to that is not what you might expect. Again, I am not here to get on a high-horse and dictate or judge. I am here to give suggestions on improvements. I believe using greed as a value system is actually inefficient. I think we can do better with a different system. In other words, I think we can actually acquire MORE under a different system.

Why do I feel greed is inefficient? Well, it is inefficient for the same reason I described competition as inefficient in the previous chapter. Greed inspires us to work AGAINST each other. Greed causes us to take more than we need. That alone on its face is inefficient. Greed sets us against each other, generates mistrust and animosity, and it creates pockets of resources piled so high that they will never be used.

It is not even the "having too much" concept that I am wanting to debate here. I have zero enthusiasm to get into political or economic philosophy arguments that make everyone angry. Someone having a lot is not the point of this discussion. The point I want to focus on is the darker side of greed. To me it is the mistrust, animosity, and competitive uncooperativeness of the whole thing. As I concluded in the last chapter, humans simply do not achieve as much using competition. Much more is accomplished if there is cooperation. Greed does not foster cooperation. Greed fosters aggressive tendencies and resentment.

What is the alternative? Love? Really? Am I crazy or something? Am I some kind of bleeding-heart delusional fool who just wants to find where the Unicorns live? No, I am not. Well, I would not mind seeing a unicorn. But I am not naïve. Thus, I am not going to just suggest we all love each other, say Namaste, and move to the next chapter. Instead let's take a look at some stuff.

I think of a value system of Love as being the same as cooperation. By "love" I mean that I care for my fellow human enough to want to help my fellow human achieve something. Instead of wanting to take from my fellow human, I want to help my fellow human. Is that because I am a nice guy? No. Oh well, I would like to think I am a nice guy, but that's not why I am doing this. I want to help my fellow human because I actually think that I and everyone else can get further ahead if we proceed under this value system.

Instead of hiding in my office and plotting how I will cause your downfall by using a variety of my costly resources to take you down, and then move in to gather all the spoils for myself, I will proceed differently. I will instead see if there is a way I can help you succeed that will also help me succeed. I believe that if I am kind to you and help you (love you), doing that will make you happier, more productive, more innovative, more efficient, AND you will see that my

142

help was invaluable to you and needed by you. Your success will open up more opportunities for me to participate in providing what I have to offer as well. Then, you can help me become more successful and achieve more things for my benefit as well. You helping me achieve success, will make me even stronger, which will then allow me to provide YOU with even more support than I was able to provide in the past. Doing that for you should make YOU more successful, which then opens up even more possibilities and opportunities for me once again. This circular motion of benefiting each other would continue to grow. We would be working together to push each other up to the top together in a cooperative manner. We would both end up at the top together, and faster than we would have otherwise.

This is in stark contrast to our present value system of greed, which is basically appealing to the lowest common denominator, and a race to the bottom, or a "one person wins, and one person loses" type scheme. Not only does that sound unpleasant and not much fun, but it guarantees that one person loses, and it does not even guarantee that the other person achieves as much as they would have wanted. With greed, there are often "costs" involved, such as bad feelings, vengeful counter-measures, and a cost in attacking your victim, and defending against attacks. It is a nasty way to live unless you have a zest for gladiator fight-to-the-death sword fights.

Under a value system of Love, we all wish each other well and help each other achieve great success together. This is not about one only giving and another only taking. This is about everyone being willing to give, and everyone ending up receiving. We each use our unique and strong gifts, talents, and skills, to CONTRIBUTE in our most efficient way.

If you have something that would make me more efficient, and I have something to make you more efficient, we cooperate and mutually provide those to each other. This helps us both grow and succeed. I can use the sappy phrase "sharing is caring" and not be too sappy because I am sharing and caring out of mutual efficiency to ensure both our successes. I am doing this because it's smarter, not because it's nicer.

But it IS nicer. Love is always nicer. That reminds me to point out that with a value system of Love, we get the benefit of avoiding the animosity, resentment, and costs associated with trying to attack our victims and defending ourselves from attacks. Instead, all of the resources get routed to the upward growth and productivity of mutual success.

Plus, there is no limit to this value system. You see, with a greed system of values, eventually your victim ends up with nothing and dies off. When that happens, there are no more victims available to take from. It is very similar to when you sheer your sheep so often that there is no wool left to sheer, and you have a sick and dying sheep. You will end up with nothing at all in the end. The greed system causes us to end up with nothing eventually. It is a game of Monopoly where only one person wins. Everyone else loses. Also, even that one person who wins will lose, because there is no society or economy to thrive in, if everyone else is destroyed. It's like having a very shiny expensive sports car, but no road to drive it on, and nobody to see how fabulous you like driving it. It becomes empty and pointless.

A value system of Love is limitless, and we as individuals, and us as a society, can continue to grow and prosper together with no end in sight. We can care about each other's well-being and success enough to foster each other to EVOLVE into something even greater. I know that if I can make you greater, that will allow you to make me greater. If I am greater, then I can help others be greater. It becomes a circular chain reaction that can spread very quickly.

Eventually, there would be a society where everyone is actively looking for ways to help each other in a mutually cooperative way. Maybe if I teach your child everything I know, that gives your child more skills, but it also gives me a new young person who might want to work with me in the future. I give them knowledge, and they give me youth, energy, and new ideas. We help each other succeed, and I have helped you, by helping your child succeed. You in turn, might be able to help me, which in turn helps your child, since they are working with me.

This concept can work and does work. I know this, because we sometimes see this kind of culture operating in small bubbles. Various communities, whether they be religious or within buildings or neighborhoods, already use some of these principles. Humans do have an appreciation for these concepts on a certain level. The problem is that we are not evolved enough as a society to move the concept to a larger broader philosophy of the masses. Human nature and old compulsions are still the majority, and that is why greed still rules.

But I think eventually, if humans evolve, they will see the wisdom in switching to a value system based upon Love. Love is better. Love is the language of God. Love IS God. Love is all we want really. Love is the best thing we can aspire to. Love is also more efficient. Love has no limits. To love is to evolve, and to evolve is to love. Plus, in the end we ALL end up with MORE.

CHAPTER EIGHTEEN

Connectivity

Connectivity is the concept that all things are related (connected) in some way. Probably many of the other books you have read might have used the spiritual phrase, "We are all one," or "We are one." You are far enough into this book to hopefully realize by now that I march to a different drum beat. I do not believe "we are all one." GASP. Instead, I believe we are all EACH individuals who are unique and have our own space of existence, spiritual being, opinions, desires, dreams, and personal boundaries of privacy and inner sanctum. We are not all one. We are infinitely many.

However, I do believe we are all "connected." I believe everything is connected. All things are connected. Now, some might argue that if all and everything is connected, then this means everything is "one," and thus, "we are one." No. There is an important distinction between everything being "one" and everything being "connected." Everything being one does not show respect for our individuality, ability to have PERSONAL BOUNDARIES from others, and our need to be independent, or more importantly, independently minded.

I am investing too much energy in advocating how important it is to not think "as one," as part of the masses, to then make it sound like "we are one," and therefore can think as one. Please let humanity never think as one. It will be independent thinking that continues to foster growth, technology, and ideas within humanity. Independent thinking also is a crucial check-and-balance against "group think" that can result in mass atrocities, delusions, and hysteria.

Okay, so we are not one, but we ARE all connected. We are connected to each other, to the Earth, and to the Universe, along with everything in it. That might seem like a boring obvious statement. But if so, then why is it that many humans behave as if they are an island unto themselves, while everyone and everything else revolves around them?

Many humans see themselves as an important institution surrounded by endless "Lazy Susans" (rotating tables) that they can simply spin at their will and take any resources they want at their whim. These are the same people who believe that trees only grow for the exclusive purpose of providing them with wood. Animals only grow to provide them with abundant food resources or amusement. Water only exists so they have something to drink, or to be used for cleansing or carrying waste away. Some people think that everything around them is only there for the sole purpose of being available for use or consumption in some way.

Some humans feel the same about people. They may look at people as cattle to be used for labor. They may see the lady who cleans as only "the lady who cleans." They may not even think of her as a person. Certainly, slavery is proof that humans have often only thought of other humans as labor and not people. This is yet another reason why I find it so important to stress the importance of individuality, and how important and special each person is. I don't like to lump people into groups so that they are "one" with the masses, and no longer a special unique person unto themselves. This type of thinking can lead to looking at masses as "cattle," or "labor," or "things," rather than special valued unique individuals.

I could easily twist this chapter into one about individual worth and value. Like, what is the value of each person? Does a person who runs a huge corporation making more money than most others, have more value than the person cleaning bathrooms? Does one person matter, and another person not so much? When one walks down the hallway, everyone looks and stares, while when another person walks by, nobody even notices the person, as if they were invisible. Yet, which person will save the life of a child they see lying on the floor sick in the bathroom? Will it be your child? If the person who cleans the bathroom is the only reason your child survives a medical incident, will you value that person more than the leader of a large corporation making millions? Who is more important?

Perhaps the leader of the corporation supports the development of a medical or safety product that will someday save the life of a loved one. Maybe it was the leader who decided to keep developing it when most others said to give up. It might be only because of that leader's choice to keep going with the product idea, that your loved one lives as a result of that product. You might really love and admire that corporate leader then, yes? You might not care about his or her financial wealth and importance, but you might be grateful they had the foresight and courage to take a risk on a product that most others would not.

Don't worry, I am sticking to a chapter on connectivity. But it is useful to see that all humans of all circumstances and backgrounds, can CONTRIBUTE in a way that affects you personally, or affects all of society. At some point or another, many of our connections to others will be revealed.

A person you have never known will end up saving your life, or the life of someone you love. You have always been connected to them in some remote way, which is impossible to see, but then when something happens, you become connected in a more direct way that becomes obvious and critically important to you. All our connections are in place already, we just cannot see most of them right now. At some point, we may see more and more of them. But there will be some connections we never actually see. That does not mean they do not exist.

Let's use the example previously alluded to, and say the person who cleans the bathrooms and discovered your child on the floor having a serious medical event, almost did not come to work that day. Perhaps they were not feeling well. But perhaps that cleaner's spouse heated up some soup for them to eat in the morning so they could feel well enough to work that day. If not for that soup being prepared and put in front of them, they never would have made it to work to find your child on the floor. Therefore, it could be said the cleaner's spouse also saved your child's life. Without the spouse, there would have been no timely rescue by the cleaner.

But that's not all. The soup was actually homemade soup brought over by the spouse's mother. So, it was "Grandma's soup." For some reason, Grandma made some soup and took the time to bring it over. If Grandma had not done that, the soup would have never been there for the spouse to serve it to the cleaner, so that the cleaner would be well enough to go to work that day and save your child. Now Grandma is a hero also.

But guess what? It turns out that Grandma is very poor and struggles for food. What had happened is that a charity organization had dropped off a ton of vegetables to Grandma. Grandma almost did not accept all the food because it was too much just for her. But she accepted it with gratitude, and just decided she would make a much larger batch of soup than she needed, so that she could bring soup over to people she thought might appreciate it. Thank goodness Grandma was given more vegetables than she needed by the charity organization.

The only reason the charity organization gave her a triple delivery of vegetables was because they had a much larger than normal donation from a big food drive that had just happened that week. The charity was afraid the vegetables would go bad, so they decided to give out triple the regular shares of vegetables.

The only reason that large food drive even happened is because one little girl at school decided to organize a community food drive as a school project. We have all seen these amazing little girls (and boys), who for one reason or another have extra gumption and are able to take the plunge and ask businesses to donate for a cause. The businesses took one look at the energetic young girl and couldn't say no. Thank goodness for that girl, and for the businesses who donated. They are heroes.

It turns out the young girl and your child are in the same grade at the same school. They know each other. If it were not for that girl, and all of the chain of events and CONNECTIVITY that she created, your child would not have been rescued in the bathroom.

So now here is the question. I wonder how your child and that girl get along. Are they friends? Or has your child teased the little girl for some reason? Did your child participate in the food drive that the girl initiated? Or did your child avoid getting involved? They are all interesting questions. However, the answers are not relevant to the fact your child was saved. Regardless of what the answers are to the above, your child still was going to be saved because that was the sequence of connected events that were caused to happen. But if your child was mean to the girl for some reason, that is an interesting karmic issue to examine. Also interesting would be if your child DID participate in the food drive. Perhaps, it was your own child's participation that resulted in the extra food donations, which down the line saved his own life. Maybe it was even your child that encouraged the girl to organize the food drive in the first place. That is connectivity. We are all connected.

Connectivity is multi-dimensional. It does not just pertain to people and events. Connectivity pertains to the Earth and the Universe. When a person throws an empty plastic bottle or candy wrapper on the ground, they do so without thinking. They don't see a nearby trash can, and they are too lazy to walk the extra distance to find a trash can, or to throw their garbage into their own vehicle. Instead, they throw it on the ground thinking it's only two little pieces of trash and maybe "a worker" will pick it up. Other people on a constant rotating basis are in the same situation and see there is trash already on the ground, and think maybe that is where everyone is throwing their trash. Thus, they all throw their trash on the ground in that area also. Since that area already has trash on the ground, they figure no harm done adding to the pile. A large area of trash on the ground grows quickly. Then there is a rain storm. All of the trash washes down the road or down a hill into a small creek bed. The trash then starts being carried by the creek down into the low-lying areas. The creek is full of trash, but the trash is moving along down the creek very quickly. The creek empties into a river, and so does all the trash. This river has many creeks full of trash that empty into it. We now have a river full of trash floating around. People are trying to go boating and fishing on this river. A month later, the person who threw the original plastic bottle and candy wrapper, is at the river trying to go boating and fishing. They are trying to avoid all the trash, and end up turning their motor off so they can clear some trash from it. They look down and see a candy wrapper and think, "Oh that's the same candy I eat." Well, yes it is, and it's also the exact same candy wrapper you threw on the ground last month.

I think you get the idea and I don't need to go on talking about how

151

the drinking water may also be polluted if some of the creeks emptied into a reservoir. Or, how the river runs into the ocean eventually, and now the ocean has infinite piles of trash in it, which are now poisoning the fish we eat, and killing ocean life.

People will say that their one or two pieces of little trash did not cause this problem. But it did. Those two first pieces of trash started the chain reaction of others thinking it was okay to drop their trash there as well. The rest is history. What would have happened if the first, second, third, and fourth person decided not to just drop their trash on the ground? What if others spoke up if they saw others dropping their trash? What if the "norm" was that everybody knew to never drop trash on the ground? That in itself is very easy and doable. It is a very contained and reasonable thing to make happen. If that were the case, no trash would have even washed into the creek to begin with. Thus, no trash into the rivers and oceans.

It starts with ONE INDIVIDUAL making the right choice. Their choice is then connected to everything else that happens after that. Everything is connected. If it was not them who found their candy wrapper floating near their boat on the river, it might have been someone they know and care about. Perhaps their Grandmother got very sick from some bad tuna or other fish that had poison in it from the ocean that had trash draining into it. We would all be sad for Grandma suffering and being sick. Maybe she even dies. Did the candy wrapper have anything to do with her poisoned fish? Maybe. Does that mean the person who dropped the candy wrapper made their own Grandmother sick, or worse? Maybe. Everything is connected. You cannot see all of the connections. Some are visible, others will be visible eventually, and some will never be visible at all. Even so, all the connections are there, whether visible or not.

What do we do with all this information and contemplation? Why is this relevant to us evolving? This is very relevant to us

152

evolving. You must realize that you have the power to influence almost anything and anybody. All of your actions, both good and bad, WILL influence others. You might see it directly, or you might see it eventually, or you may never personally see it. But you are influencing the lives of others through your decisions and actions.

How many of us have had that one teacher or mentor who never realized how much of a huge impact they had on our lives? That teacher or mentor made decisions and actions that had a large impact on others, for which they may have no knowledge of for the most part. Just because they never saw the result does not mean there was no result. Being evolved means understanding that previous sentence.

When we make a choice or do something, the evolved person will think to themselves, "I don't know who this will affect, but it will have an effect on someone." Therefore, consider if you want to initiate good effects or bad effects. Do you want to start positive chain reactions, or negative chain reactions? Do you want to be the little girl who started the food drive that actually saved the other child lying on the floor in the bathroom? Do you want to be Grandma who was nice enough to bring over the hot soup that actually allowed the cleaner to go to work and save the child? Just like the little girl and Grandma, you do not know what your impact will be through your choices and actions. However, the result of your choices and actions might be life altering to someone. You might not only save a life, but end up changing the world. Perhaps the child that was saved in the bathroom ends up becoming someone who saves even more lives someday. If that happens, it would only be thanks to all those who caused him to be saved that day in the bathroom.

As an evolved person, realize that however big or small you feel in this world, you have the same value and importance as anyone else. Your choices and actions could become the most important of anyone's in your community. You might be that one person at the beginning of the chain that does what needs to be done so that

153

something important and amazing can happen later on. It is possible you will never even realize your connection to that specific important thing. But know that everything is connected, and thus you are connected to everything.

To an evolved mind, this concept goes far beyond other people and the land around us. This concept reaches to the stars. Your goodwill reaches others out there you don't even know. Your prayers for people you don't even know, and perhaps the prayers for others on other planets, can be heard and felt. One ACTION of goodwill can and will impact the UNIVERSE in some way.

Being the odd person that I am, I often have dreams of people who seem deceased to me, but they are in my dreams and my mind, as if trying to connect with me. I do not fear them. I listen to them. I hear them. If they seem in pain, I provide comfort to them in my dream. When I wake up, it is always my hope that I have provided some comfort to some spiritual soul that needed it. Perhaps that soul belongs to someone here on Earth who can't sleep because they fear their deceased loved one is not at peace. Perhaps me giving comfort in this dream of mine, can give comfort to someone's deceased loved one, which can then give comfort and peace to someone alive and mourning in pain. I do not know who any of these people are. Or do I? We will never know. But I know we are all connected, here, and there. Everywhere. I know everything is connected, whether it be between humans, animals, the Earth, the sky, or spirits in Heaven. I know my choices and actions will cause an eventual result, and I want that result to be positive.

Please join me, all who wish to evolve, and do the same in making choices and actions that will result in something positive, even if we never see it ourselves. That is what evolved people do.

CHAPTER NINETEEN

First Contact

I am hoping we do not need to spend much time arguing over whether or not there is other intelligent life in the Universe besides humans on Earth. If you promise not to argue with me over that, then I will promise not to debate over exactly how "intelligent" humans really are. The Universe is a huge place beyond anyone's comprehension. The amount of other intelligent life out there would be nearly infinite. That was me upping the stakes from "there is other intelligent life," to "the amount of other intelligent life out there would be nearly infinite."

Think of it this way. Even today, there are new species being discovered here on Earth. Think about that. Humans have been here on Earth for how long? And we are still discovering species of life on this planet that we never discovered before? This is just here on

Earth. Imagine what we could have missed right here in our own solar system. Now consider the number of solar systems out there. Does anyone know? No, but the number of solar systems in the Universe is so big that we don't have a number for it. So, if I told you there were countless trillions of solar systems, that would be a major understatement. To say the number of solar systems is "countless" would be more accurate.

Based on that, I think the chances are fair that there might even be other beings very similar to humans out there somewhere. In fact, there might even be other humans of our same species out there on a different planet in a different solar system. Again, consider the fact that here on Earth, it is not uncommon for people to discover late in life that they have a brother or sister they never knew about. If that can happen routinely on Earth, then why can't we have a sister or brother species of humans out there in the Universe someplace. They possibly live on a planet very similar to Earth.

Of course, the catch is that we are not as likely to bump into another human civilization because humans really struggle with having technology necessary for fast deep-space travel. It would depend on whether this other human civilization has evolved differently than us. Our civilization has been based upon greed, and being totally consumed with competing and conquering each other. That type of behavior distracts us from focusing, cooperating, and achieving great technological advances necessary for deep-space travel.

But perhaps our sister or brother human civilization evolved under a different set of values and priorities. If their civilization was based upon total cooperation and harmony, they likely have achieved technological advances beyond our imagination. Thus, perhaps they might find US, even if we are not able to find them.

However, it is more likely that the first alien species we make contact with, will be very different from humans. They are probably adapted to a different planetary environment, and thus they would look very different from humans, and have different attributes. They may or may not have a humanoid type body form. Perhaps they are tiny creatures, or huge creatures. Maybe they don't even have eyes. Humans love assuming that every other creature in the Universe is going to be somewhat similar to them. The truth is that we have no idea.

I have drawn up this discussion the way I have on purpose. I have laid out the possibility that other intelligent life out there may be humans just like us. But I have also laid out the possibility that other intelligent life out there are so different from us that we cannot even comprehend what strange forms they might take. It could be either of those, or anything in the middle, or perhaps something far outside the parameters I set. I am open to the possibility that the truth is actually a paradox, or something so beyond comprehension that it cannot be mentally defined. What could be outside my parameters of humans on one hand, or completely weird creatures on the other hand? Well, the intelligent life might not be a flesh inhabiting organic creature at all. Perhaps the intelligent life is an energy force that has no form at all. Perhaps it just consists of intelligent energy molecules.

When we start talking like this, about "intelligent energy," it brings me back to my thoughts about human souls after the human body dies. My belief has always been that the body dies, but the soul lives on in the form of intelligent energy that returns back "Home" "to God" "in Heaven" "in the Universe." You can apply whatever your spiritual or religious beliefs are, but if the soul lives on, then it means there is intelligent energy out there. Is that "intelligent energy" considered "intelligent life?"

Could it be that a human dies and transforms into a different "life form," which could be described as another type of "intelligent life?" Perhaps this intelligent life can travel at will, including to other civilizations in the Universe. Would that make them alien visitors? Perhaps, we the humans, after our body dies, are aliens in the form of our "soul of energy," visiting other civilizations. But that would be in the context of an energy force being considered a life form. I am not here to tell you what to think. I am just presenting some ideas for you to contemplate. Interestingly, many of these ideas are not totally inconsistent with some spiritual and religious beliefs.

For example, those who believe when we die our soul goes to be with God, well, that means our soul life force is wherever God is. Where is God? In Heaven? In the Universe? Are there other life forms in Heaven or the Universe? Is God only for humans, or for all life? How universal is God? I don't know. The answer to that question is defined by your own personal religious and spiritual views, or lack thereof. I will leave that to you. I also realize plenty of people have views that are not even relevant to any discussion of God and Heaven. Some might believe that humans do not even have souls, thus there is no energy force. I do not have proof. All I have are my own beliefs, just like you have your own beliefs. I respect all beliefs because I cannot prove one to be right, or one to be wrong. Thus, an open mind is the prudent position to take.

Back to aliens. I would be remiss if I didn't discuss that the aliens we might have first contact with could be the "grey" aliens with the famous big eyes and little humanoid bodies. We have all been raised to believe that this is what an alien looks like. Why is this? Who knows. Maybe we indeed already captured or recovered an alien body. Or perhaps as humans, we have these self-manufactured notions of what certain things are supposed to look like. Or perhaps some among us have seen them.

I will tell you this much for sure. Whatever form these aliens arrive in, we know one thing for certain. The aliens will be more advanced than humans. This might be the only thing we can rely on as a stipulated fact. The reason why is because in order for an alien species to find us, they must have developed the ability for deep-space travel. That ability is beyond our human capabilities. Thus, the aliens would be very advanced to accomplish this. Thus, we all should agree right now that we will be dealing with a life form that is far advanced beyond humans.

Let us now move forward and set up a scenario where a "first contact" event happens. An alien lands on Earth with a ship or transporter device. What does this mean? Again, we must go with the assumption that the alien is far more advanced, and thus more intelligent, than humans. With that in mind, we have to assume that the alien's arrival has been very well thought out and planned. The alien will have done incredible amounts of research about Earth and humans. The alien will know everything about us and our capabilities before arriving. So, they will know everything about us, while we know nothing about them.

Additionally, we have to assume the alien has some sort of motive for arriving, otherwise it would be a pointless use of resources and risk. So, what is their motive? Your guess is as good as mine. Their motive could be to make a first contact in order to begin a communication, relationship, or some kind of exchange.

Their motive could be for research purposes. Perhaps they have completed all the research, and gained all the knowledge they could without having contact with us. Therefore, now they MUST make contact in order to further their research. Humans do the same thing with animals. We can observe them in nature, but eventually we like to interact with the animal so that we can see how it will behave toward us personally. Aliens would be having the same thoughts perhaps, and need direct contact to see how we will react to them personally.

Have you considered the idea that all of the alleged UFO sightings and human abduction stories could be the process of "research" that I was speaking of earlier? It could be the aliens doing all of the possible research they can without having a "first contact" moment. Their research methods all these years could be them leading up to a first contact moment when they feel they are ready.

But are humans ready? What would humans do if an alien arrived on Earth for that first contact moment? What would happen if a human got into a cage with a tiger? Would the tiger ignore the human? Would the tiger run and hide? Or would the tiger attack and eat the human? We are not sure, are we? It often depends on the mood of the tiger. Tigers are very unpredictable. I would suggest to you that aliens would think of us as a tiger. They would look at us as a less advanced, lower thinking, unpredictable creature.

Therefore, the alien would be wondering if it is a good idea to "step inside a cage" with a human. Humans have a horrible history and habit of killing first, and asking questions later. Why would an alien arrive and make contact if they can predict with some accuracy that the chances of the humans trying to kill them are pretty high? I do not think I am being unreasonable with my assumption that there is a high probability that humans WOULD react to an alien with fear and violence. A human would be scared for certain. When humans are scared, they have the "fight or flight" reflex. When a human cannot take flight, they will fight. A human would likely want to try and capture the alien if they can, but if that is not possible, they would think to kill the alien. Maybe I am just in a cynical mood as I write this, but my own observations of humans tell me I am not far off the truth.

Under those probable conditions, why would an alien attempt contact? They likely would not. That is precisely why we might not have had a universally known and accepted "first contact" moment yet. Of course, there may have already been some human and alien contact that has not been spoken of publicly. Some humans may have already had direct or indirect contact with aliens, but will not discuss it. Or, if they have discussed it, they are discredited as being crazy, and not believed.

Here is my suspicion. I believe aliens are trying to prepare humans for first contact. I believe aliens have allowed us to see UFOs, and I believe aliens have had some sort of contact with certain humans that they believed would be no threat to them. I believe the aliens have a "conditioning program" they are operating, meaning that they are gradually exposing humans to their existence over time so that humans will become accepting of their existence. If humans are accepting of alien existence, then humans are less likely to freak out and be violent.

In the next chapter I am going to discuss the idea of "aliens" already being among us here on Earth. This is consistent with my theory that aliens are gathering research, and trying to condition humans to the idea of their existence. But I don't want to get ahead of myself.

Let us now assume that the alien feels the humans they are about to present themselves to will not immediately attempt to harm them. The alien will likely appear before a human or group of humans that it has researched. It probably will not be a random accident of who the alien makes first contact with. The alien will be hoping this particular group of humans will not be violent, and will be open and able to handle a first contact moment.

Once the alien appears before the humans, what will happen next? I think it is a reasonable assumption that the alien will very quickly make the first move in the form of some sort of "offering" or opening statement. It seems likely to me that the alien will have learned our language and can make a statement in our own language. However, this assumes they have mouths that can speak. What if they don't?

If for some reason the alien can't speak, or speak in our language, they will offer some sort of sign that they come in peace, and identify with us in some way. Let's go back to the tiger analogy. If a human is going to go into the cage with the tiger, a human might try a couple of tactics. First, a human might give the tiger some food. Maybe throw the tiger some steaks until it is satisfied and no longer immediately hungry. Smart, yes? After the human feels the tiger will not immediately eat him, the human might then bravely offer a hand (not to eat), but a hand for the tiger to smell and realize the human is not going to hurt him. Perhaps the human will then try to pet the tiger.

The alien thinks of humans like humans think of the tiger. So, what is the alien likely to do? Well, the alien will likely make some kind of offering to satisfy and calm us humans. What might that be? In my thinking it might be something very familiar and identifiable to humans. Remember, the aliens would have done their research and would know everything about humans before the pioneer alien arrives. I would guess that the alien might start playing some music we are familiar with. Who could be afraid of an alien that introduces itself by playing something from The Beetles? Yes, it is silly, but it's also brilliant. I believe the alien will be brilliant in its approach. If I was advising the alien, I would suggest this approach. A more cynical approach would be for the alien to make an offering of money. They would know how human civilization is based upon money and greed. Someone on the alien advisory board would most certainly make this very valid but crass suggestion. You get the idea.

We would have an immediate offering of some sort. Secondly, we would have some sort of structured statement of communication. We do not know if this communication would come in the form of spoken words, written words, or perhaps in some other method. Many humans are becoming very developed in empathic thinking, and even are working toward at least partial telepathic communication. Perhaps the alien would be sure one of the humans present would be one of these humans who can sense their thoughts empathically. Perhaps the alien would try to communicate telepathically through this human interpreter who could at least understand some of the alien's thoughts.

I suspect the initial communication would contain the alien's desire to calm the humans and express the alien's intent. What would we do with the tiger? We would calm the tiger and try to show the tiger that we only want to examine it, touch it, or watch it. We would do this by not making any sudden threatening movements. We would likely only use our hands, and show the tiger our hands were empty. I would expect the same from the alien.

What next? The answer to this will go back to the alien's motive for making the first contact. In my book, *Aliens: The Alien Agenda*, I go into great detail regarding my theories of why aliens are so fascinated with humans, and what their motives may be. But for the sake of our little discussion here, if their motive was only to introduce themselves and observe our reaction, they would be ready to leave as soon as they have accomplished this. When we are in the cage with the tiger, we are most certainly not going to stay in there long or take a nap in there, right? We are going to have our moment of contact, and then get the heck out of there.

I believe the alien will do the same thing. The alien will accomplish their mission, and then they will leave as quickly and efficiently as they arrived. At that point, they would let us digest what just happened, and they would observe our behavior and attitudes toward the first contact. Our reaction to the first contact would then dictate how additional events of contact go, or if there is any further personal contact at all.

As humans, we would be flummoxed as to why they came, what they wanted, when we are going to be fully invaded, and how many weapons we need to prepare for the next arrival. Humans would wonder why the alien bothered to show up, why was the meeting so short, and why did the alien not stay. I have already answered all of these questions in a very logical way. The problem is that humans as a whole are not logical. My fear is that humans will not be able to logically reason their way through the first contact in an accurate way. I think the aliens will know this also, and thus will wait some time before they come again. However, if the visit went well, we might see other visits in different and unpredictable ways that are safe for the aliens, and perhaps constructive and calming to humans.

It is not an accident that this chapter is further back in the book. The reason is that humans will have to evolve to a certain level before a first contact moment is possible. So far in this book, we have discussed the need for humans to eliminate their fears, stop false thinking, think in a more logical way, and to develop better communication skills. Pretty much everything we discussed in this book needs to be embraced by humans before humans are truly ready for alien interaction that is safe for both aliens and humans. Aliens are likely waiting patiently for this evolution to happen. This means both aliens and humans have something significant in common, and are waiting for the same thing. They are both waiting for humans to evolve.

CHAPTER TWENTY

Aliens Among Us?

In the previous chapter we discussed what an alien "first contact" moment might look like. The ironic thing is that we might have already had contact with aliens. We previously discussed how aliens would be much more advanced than humans, and would be doing an abundance of research on humans, Earth, and who knows what else.

I think the first thing we need to do is define what an "alien" might be in the context of this particular discussion. I should say first that I do not think little grey men with big eyes are hiding inside someone's barn in Idaho or someplace. This is not like in the Steven Spielberg movie *ET*, where a strange alien creature is going to wear lots of clothing, draped in a hoodie, and then go out grocery shopping without being noticed.

I think any alien presence before a full first contact moment is going to be in the form of a human, an energy presence, or combination thereof. I think it will be interesting to watch scientific advancements regarding DNA research. I think many people wonder if it is possible that some kind of alien existence might be factored into our DNA somehow. There are plenty of anecdotal stories of people being abducted, and there being some sort of fertility experiments conducted during the abduction. Of course, there is no proof of this, but there are plenty of independent claims of it happening.

Another possibility is that aliens have been able to create a new race of themselves that are in a human form. There are plenty of people on this planet with questionable parentage. This might be harder to pull off in countries like The United States with very tight record keeping and information controls, but there are plenty of other places in the world where a person could exist without any clear birth records of who both parents are.

Yet another possibility, is that aliens exist among us in the form of a "consciousness" within some of us. What would happen if an alien consciousness entered a human body? Would you call that a "possession?" I call it a "walk-in." Each person can believe what they want, but I believe it is very possible that aliens exist among us in the form of an "alien consciousness" within some humans.

What about an alien presence being in the form of animals? Humans are so fixated on aliens vs. humans, but what if the alien presence is within animals? How would we know? Does anyone here dispute how "alien" and "superior" cats seem to behave? The truth is that humans cannot even anticipate what form an alien might take. Humans are left to make endless assumptions, most of which might be wrong.

I feel there is a high likelihood that there is some kind of alien presence already among us on Earth. Notice I said "among us on Earth." I am not counting any alien presence that could be hidden

166

away within some mountain range on Earth, or perhaps on the dark side of the moon, or maybe even Mars. For our purposes, we are discussing an alien presence here on Earth within our general population. You might have already come into direct contact with an alien presence and not even realized it.

Regardless of whether the alien form consists of some kind of partial DNA replacement, clone, test-tube baby, or foreign consciousness within a human mind, how might we recognize an alien presence? Clearly, we would not know an alien when we see one. Would there be any way to tell?

To answer this question, we need to consider what would make an alien different from a human. We know we cannot really tell from a physical perspective under our current scenario. Perhaps someday there will be some kind of DNA test or brain scan that could tell us. But for now, there seems no physical way to test for this, even if you want to assume for a moment that there IS an alien presence among us.

That leaves us with trying to discern alien existence among us through behavioral observation. How might aliens act differently than humans? Obviously, we need to go back to the root motivation for an alien species to even want to infiltrate a human civilization. We assumed it would be for research purposes. There might be some unknown purpose or goal beyond the research, but whatever their ultimate goal is, intense research of humans and Earth would be the first order of business.

If the motive for infiltrating a human population is research, then we can expect an alien presence to be very curious and observant. We can rule out the obnoxious loud humans that talk too much and never listen, because they think they know everything. I can guarantee you an alien would NOT behave THAT WAY. An alien would be more likely to be totally silent actually. An alien does not need to prove anything. An alien simply wants to gain information for research.

167

An alien would likely seem very intelligent and advanced. This would be evident in both their mental intellect as well as their behavior. Aliens would probably not have all the emotional and behavioral shortcomings that humans have. An alien won't be acting impulsively on emotion, or be exhibiting other common behaviors such as fear.

In a nutshell, you could expect an alien to act "evolved," perhaps as outlined in this book. An alien would appear to be a human who is very evolved, quiet, curious, and highly intelligent. Who around you are this way? I am laughing, and I hope you are too. Of course, the funny and scary part is that I might not be joking. We can only contemplate and guess.

Incidentally, I am sure I am not alone in noticing that over the years, an increasing number of children seem to exhibit the traits I describe. Many kids are being described as "different," but also possess some advanced traits of increased sensitivity to the surroundings around them. There are many kids among the high functioning "autistic" population, and with Aspergers, who while showing signs of the disorders, also show signs of gifted brilliance. Science is still trying to determine what exactly causes these disorders. I am not for a moment suggesting that everyone with Autism and Aspergers is an alien. I am only pointing out there are some mysterious disorders we cannot fully explain, where people have social disorders, but also some "different" features of thinking and observation. For example, I would never assume a child that lives in his own world is not gifted. Perhaps that is EXACTLY the type of child who is gifted in a special way. Again, I am not suggesting these disorders suggest anything alien. They are examples of human "disorders" where some humans who are afflicted with the "disorders," are still at the same time quite unusually gifted or unique in certain ways. By the way, I believe all humans are gifted in some special way. An evolved person never underestimates anybody, regardless of any apparent disorder or disability. It might be that these folks are some of the most gifted in ways we do not all see or recognize.

Now that we have described what an alien presence might look like in real life, the next question would be, what do we do about this? I would recommend doing nothing. First of all, we will not go around suggesting someone is alien without proof. We will not make accusations without proof. That would be immoral and wrong on every level.

But let's say and it is true and some people have an alien component. Is that their fault? Does that make them bad in some way? Humans are naturally afraid of things they do not understand, and have that fight or flight instinct. There is nothing to be afraid of in my thinking, because there is nothing we can do about it anyway. Also, if harm was going to come from this, it would have already happened most likely.

Let's revisit the tiger analogy. If the tiger suspects something is going on, and he is being observed for some odd reason, what should the tiger do? Should the tiger just attack and eat everyone watching him? Or should the tiger accept all the great food offerings and just keep living its routines as long as nobody causes it harm? Just like the tiger, it would be illogical to attack and eat everyone observing us, without direct cause, reason, or purpose. Let's be like the tiger. I like the tiger.

But that leaves us with one last question I want to explore. If there IS an alien presence among us already, why don't the aliens just come out and make themselves known? Based upon the discussions of the previous chapter, as well as this one, the answer should be somewhat obvious. Clearly, it would not be logical or safe for aliens to make themselves known yet. Most humans are not evolved enough to handle a healthy interaction with aliens yet. Humans can't even accept other humans with different physical differences and races. Imagine how humans would react to species not even of this planet when they can't even handle different races of themselves on their own home planet. It is just simply a bad idea for any aliens to expose themselves and their identity at this time.

If you are someone who wants aliens to come out and show themselves, then be someone who exhibits acceptance of all your fellow humans first. After humans can accept different humans, we can look at the possibility of humans being ready to accept species from other planets. Let's evolve.

For those with a particular interest in aliens, their likely psychology, society, spaceship technology, and culture, I would suggest you take a look at my book, *Aliens: The Alien Agenda*. I go into much deeper detail regarding aliens, whereas in this book we will remain focused on evolving, and evolve we will.

CHAPTER TWENTY-ONE

Everyone Is Psychic

My own belief is that everyone is psychic. I know that is quite a statement to make, and might cause some gasps and groans. Why is that? Well, some people view psychics as crazy people who wear tinfoil hats. Worse yet, some think psychics are heretics living submerged within the occult, which is located right next to Satan's vacation home. People think psychics are charlatans who have lost their marbles, or are just trying to steal everyone else's marbles.

On the other side of the bleachers, plenty of others view psychics as these mystical guides who indeed have these mysterious powers and must certainly be either aliens, possessed by entities, or perhaps are living partly in the spirit world and partly on Earth. Psychic abilities are viewed as magical and amazing powers that for some reason are gifted upon a few because they are "special." Or maybe, psychic abilities were just bestowed on people who stuck their finger in a light socket when they were young (please nobody actually do this, sigh).

The first paragraph is completely false, while the second paragraph is partly false. I don't believe those with psychic abilities are evil heretics drinking vodka with Satan. As for the second paragraph, yes, it is true I stuck a coat hanger wire into an electrical outlet when I was 7 or so. It made a big noise and scared the crap out of me. My mother never found out, so please don't tell her. But I digress. I doubt it had much to do with my abilities, other than cause me to make some bad life choices along the way. Okay, I must stop digressing.

Our first order of business will be to clear up this idea of psychics and psychic ability. Not everyone is a psychic. What I said was that everyone is psychic. A psychic is someone who wears their psychic ability as a name tag on their chest and considers it to be their job, or even identity. Meanwhile, people who are psychic, consider their psychic ability as just one of their many attributes, like being smart, tall, short, or funny.

I have been wrestling with these labels for a long time now. People who don't want to be identified as wearing a tinfoil hat call themselves "intuitive." But being intuitive has meant that the person is less than psychic. I think most considered me intuitive my entire life. But later in life, I was identified and labeled as being "a psychic," and I had to wear that tinfoil hat. While some were mildly impressed, others thought I was crazy (and still do). I have come to the conclusion that I do not like any of the labels. Even being labeled with great abilities has its problems. I was once listed in some publication as one of the 50 top psychics in the world. This became a problem because there was an expectation that I could tell you what color underwear you had on that day, and that I could tell you what would happen to you tomorrow, and when your ex-boyfriend Tommy would finally magically come back to you, even though he was never coming back to you. I am not a circus bear who does tricks, and those were not specific questions or skills I wished to be tested on every day.

Thus, the bottom line is that I no longer like being identified as a psychic. I prefer to be considered a person who has psychic ability. It is one of my many attributes that make up who I am. It is not my identity. I am psychic to a certain degree just like you are. Yes, that's right. We have that in common, you and me. We are both psychic.

You might be thinking, "Umm no." Well, I didn't say you all had highly developed psychic ability at this moment, nor did I say you choose to use your psychic ability. I just said you are psychic, meaning you have psychic ability within you. Some of you who have more developed psychic ability know it, own it, and sell it. Some of you have developed your psychic ability already, but don't wish to fully engage. You admit it to those around you, or perhaps you have kept it secret because tinfoil hats don't suit your fashion style.

In my view, psychic ability is similar to mathematics. All humans have the potential and ability to do both. Some people are naturally gifted at math and seem brilliant with it. Others can get through math okay as long as they pay attention in class and study hard. Others are terrible at math and mostly need a calculator (like me). But all humans can do math to some degree.

Just like math, all humans CAN use psychic ability, but some people are better at it than others. Additionally, those who spend time working on developing their psychic ability tend to be "more psychic" than others who don't spend any effort to develop their psychic ability. People who study math and practice tend to be better at math. People who study psychic ability and practice it, tend to be more developed with their psychic ability.

Psychic ability is something all humans can develop. Some will, and some won't. Some will work on it, and others might purposely choose not to develop it. It is a personal choice. Your level of psychic ability is very much in your control. Yes, some are more gifted than others, but the same is true with math, music, sports, and everything else humans are capable of.

We have to stop this notion of "psychics" being above or below everyone else. People who are psychic are just like you. God did not one day "knight them" with a sword on their shoulder, and conversely, psychics are not crazy evil heretics to be avoided. Yes, there ARE some crazy psychics out there who love their tinfoil hats, BUT there are also lots of crazy mathematicians out there who love wearing a bow tie. For the most part, most of us fall in the middle someplace. We have to remove all the weird stigmas related to psychic ability. It's the evolved thing to do.

Okay. So, if we established that everyone has psychic ability to some degree, and only needs to develop it, then why doesn't everyone develop it? Why haven't more people exhibited their psychic ability? I have an answer. The reason is that in order to develop your naturally engrained psychic ability, you must open up your senses to a much higher degree than you presently do, and you must lose your fear of what might happen if you do this.

Most humans are too uncomfortable and afraid to develop their psychic ability. Psychic ability is an evolved ability and skill. Like all evolved skills, it requires CHANGING how you think. You must open your psyche, senses, "psychic gates," or however you want to refer to it. This means making yourself more vulnerable to what may come your way. Does this mean a closet full of ghosts and demons can fly inside your head if you open yourself up? Are you taking a huge risk? No, I am not referring to any of that. I am referring to the fact that psychic messages can evoke deep feelings within you, and bring messages you might not expect. You have to yield control of your senses enough to accept the messages and feelings that might be out there.

I will attempt to explain this better, but to be honest, it is much like trying to explain to someone who has never had sex, what having sex

174

is like. And like having sex, developing your psychic ability is something you should only do when you are mature enough and ready. With that said, let me explain the different components I think are necessary to understand this. Also, I preface my descriptions with the warning that I am very much over simplifying what psychic ability is. I am trying to do this in one chapter rather than an entire book. So bear with me.

For me, the basics of psychic ability are generally and roughly based upon the following principles:

1. Empathy
2. Opening senses
3. Listening

But before I get to that, let me first explain what I think psychic ability is. Everything within us and around us consists of energy. If you will go along with the belief that we have eternal souls, then that soul itself consists of energy. Everything on Earth and in the Universe is surrounded by, and consists of, energy.

Energy gives off frequencies. You have the energy/entities that give off a signal, and you have energy/entities that can receive the signal. Everything that consists of energy, is living, thinks, or acts, gives off energy frequencies. This would be like a radio station broadcasting to you through their radio frequency.

Then you have the entity that can receive the frequencies. That would be the radio itself, as well as you and me. The radio can pick up the radio station frequency if it is tuned in correctly. You can also pick up frequencies if you tune in correctly. In essence, you are a radio tuning into certain energies and frequencies, and trying to pick up the music, information, and messages that you can listen to if you are correctly tuned into the desired frequency.

Psychic ability is training your senses so that you can tune into the

175

frequencies you want, receive the frequencies, and then listen to the information carried on those frequency waves. Again, I don't have scientific astrophysics data to show you, and I am being simplistic. This is also my own simplified view of how it works, and others will have other theories that might be equally as valid. Other professional opinions are good and valid.

So now let us discuss how to build your ability to pick up those energy frequencies. We are now going back to the list of those three items: empathy, opening senses, and listening. Psychic ability is based upon empathy because you need to be able to FEEL everything around you. Empathy is our ability to feel emotions of others as if you were experiencing them yourself. Remember, sympathy is just your ability to feel sorry for someone experiencing something. Empathy is you actually feeling it with them as if you were actually them.

The first step in developing psychic ability is to build your sense of empathy. This requires you to focus in on someone (tune in), and then feel (sense) what they are feeling or putting out for energy frequencies. People-watching is a great way to practice this. Look at a person, observe them carefully, and put yourself in their shoes. Try to guess what they are thinking and feeling. You would be surprised how good you can become at this if you practice.

The downside to empathy is that you subject yourself to feeling other people's pain. This is precisely why many people choose to shut it off and not open themselves up. Conversely, some people have very little empathy, or choose to not engage their empathy. These people are the least psychic people on Earth. You cannot have psychic ability if you do not have empathy.

So let's say you are able to engage with a high level of empathy so that you can feel others and everything around you. The next step would be to open your senses. This is more difficult to describe. Basically, you have to CHOOSE to hear, see, and feel everything around you using intent. Opening your senses means making a conscious choice to pick up all stimuli into your senses that might come your way. This is like a radio desperately trying to receive a station. The radio is able, willing, and wanting to receive any stations it possibly can. To do that, you as a person need to be able, willing, and wanting to SENSE anything that comes your way.

The best way to practice opening your senses might be to meditate in different settings. This allows you to train your mind to relax and completely open to whatever what may come your way. If you are successful, you will start to pick up on things you never picked up on before. You should be able to sense small changes in room temperature, where before you would have ignored it and tuned it out as being irrelevant. When you open your senses, EVERYTHING becomes relevant. You want to pick up on everything.

Another key point of trying to sense things, is to train your mind to become IN ALIGHMENT with whatever you are trying to pick up. This is hard to explain, but as with empathy, you are trying to BECOME what you are tuning into.

Once you show the willingness and ability to fully open up your senses, the next step is to develop the skill of Listening. Once your senses are open, you must LISTEN. This is like after a radio has tuned into a station, and now you listen to whether it is a song, news broadcast, what exact song, or what they exactly they are discussing on the news.

The best way to describe listening, is to remind you what it's like to not listen. All of us have turned on the TV or radio out of habit, but then we get distracted and are not even listening to what is happening on the radio or TV. We have no idea what show is on, or what the commercial is talking about. We are not listening. We have it tuned in. We hear it. But we are not listening.

Listening is when we carefully pay attention to what information, feelings, or impressions we are receiving. It is best to listen in a very literal sense. Many psychics will tell you that they often receive messages that do not make sense to them at the time. A good listener will accurately remember the message, even if it does not make sense. A bad listener will twist the message into something that makes more sense to them, or even worse, something they want to hear. A bad psychic only gives messages we want to hear, rather than the truth of what is actually heard. Truth comes when you listen carefully and take the message as it is. You can contemplate the message later, and try to interpret what it means to you, but it is important to use the original accurate literal message that was received.

What about those psychics who claim to communicate with dead people? Can you do that also? Yes. Remember earlier in the book I promised to teach you how to do this? We have arrived. I will remind you though, that just because you CAN communicate with the deceased, does not mean you WILL, or that you will WANT to. A person should only develop abilities they are comfortable and ready for. I also want to respect anyone's religious views who are against this. I respect your religious values, and it is totally fine if you choose not to engage in this part of the discussion. I only ask that you save your hate mail, and respect my ability to discuss this topic with others who are interested. We are all different, with different values and opinions. We can co-exist without throwing things at each other.

Let us proceed. Communicating with a deceased person can be tricky. First of all, you must "tune into" a very specific channel, meaning that specific person. Secondly, you have to realize that even if you tune in correctly, you might not receive or hear anything.

If you believe in souls of energy that move onto a different realm of existence, you also have to believe that the energy has a choice in whether it communicates (sends a signal) or not. We cannot force a spirit to communicate. Please also realize that having an active communication with a deceased person is very different from picking up on RESIDUAL "ghost energy" in an old house or room. Picking up on residual energy is simply tuning into old energy with old

178

frequencies. It is like listening to an old tape of someone speaking. It is not real time. What we are attempting to do here is communicate in real time with a deceased person's spirit.

The best way to tune into the person is to use some sort of personal aide that helps you tune in. For me, it is very often a clear photo of the person where I can see their eyes. A personal belonging from that person is also very useful. Each person needs to discover what works best for them. If developing psychic ability was like doing math, then communicating with the deceased is like learning to sing. A person learning to sing has to find their own way to a degree, and your voice is either pretty good, or you sound like a frog like me. This is why "Mediumship," or communicating with deceased people is a more advanced skill that not everyone is able to develop at a high level. Not every psychic is a Medium, and not every person can sing very well, or be a very good Medium.

However, everyone is allowed to try. So, hold onto the person's personal item, or stare at their picture. You want to tune into that "channel" or "frequency." Next, use your skills in proper order. Turn your empathy scale up to maximum. Try to FEEL the person through the personal item. Then, open all your senses as wide open as you possibly can. After that, LISTEN carefully for any kind of message or impression. You can ask a question or mentally send out an intent. You may or may not be able to receive anything. This takes a lot of skill and practice, and some natural ability like singing does.

Also realize that this might be a very upsetting exercise for you. If you are trying to communicate with a dear loved one that you are mourning, it might be too overwhelming. By definition, you must make yourself completely vulnerable and open during this process. Many who are mourning and trying to keep themselves together will have trouble doing this until they are more stable. This is precisely why people will hire a skilled psychic Medium who can do this objectively and calmly, with practiced skill.

I am including this skill in the form of a teaching lesson because I feel many people would benefit from reaching some sort of skill level with this. Maybe you won't be the world's greatest psychic medium, but if you can connect to your loved one so that you can actually feel them, and maybe even get some brief messages, my hope is that this gives you some peace, comfort, and happiness. This exercise is not about making you cry harder or feel miserable. This is an optional skill to develop if it will bring some peace into your life and help you with your loss. Plus, I promised earlier I would teach you. At the very least, you have a better understanding of how it all works.

Is psychic ability dangerous? It is probably equally dangerous as driving a car is. If you are irresponsible and reckless, you can drive off the road and hurt yourself. But if you carefully, pay attention, and learn well, you will be fine. The biggest thing to remember with psychic ability is that you can and should shut it down whenever you feel it is out of control or you feel uncomfortable.

I am not going to spend this chapter or book talking about all the different kinds of spirits, guides, angels, demons, and so forth. I discuss all of this in greater detail within my book *The Hunter Equation*. I did warn you that this topic was going to be general and over-simplified. Obviously, there is much more to discuss, with many side-topics to cover.

I am not telling everyone to become super-psychics and try to let every spirit or demon of the Universe into their head. Again, save the hate mail. This was a very important chapter and topic that had to be included in this book. The reason is because psychic ability is something all evolved humans will develop eventually. All humans already have the potential ability within them. It's there already. It is only a matter of time before more and more humans decide to fully develop their abilities. Therefore, it is important we acknowledge that, and give you all a chance to start contemplating your feelings on the issue.

Some of you will prefer to let others be the psychics and the mathematicians, while others of you might want to start exploring and learning more about your abilities. Some of this is like singing, in that it's best to practice in private before subjecting others to sounds of a frog, and subjecting yourself to embarrassment. I promise you that nobody will ever catch me singing. However, I still love music and love learning about it.

As I said, everyone is psychic. I respect your abilities as much as I respect your choice to use them or not. Do not let anyone tell you that you cannot do something, or that they have God-given gifts you don't have. God gives us all gifts. It is up to each of us to use them or not. Let us all evolve and explore our gifts.

CHAPTER TWENTY-TWO

Super Powers

I do not think humans are going to evolve into Superman or Spiderman. I don't think humans will develop X-ray vision that can also pierce buildings with lasers shooting from our eyes. When I speak of super powers, I am not referring to physical attributes that are simply not in our DNA.

When I speak of super powers, I am more referring to mental abilities that we have yet to realize are even there. Humans use a small percentage of their brain. In fact, I swear some humans don't use any of their brain, but let's not go there. However, some humans, such as Albert Einstein, seemed to possess mental abilities far beyond the average human.

My own brush with psychic abilities has convinced me there is so much more up there in that empty space in my head than I thought there was. While I have done my fair share of really stupid things, I have also experienced senses, sensations, and "information" that were unexpected and unexplained. It is one thing to remember facts, but it is another to actually SENSE things.

I have noticed my own mental ability is divided up into different abilities that feel as if they come from different universes within my head. Depending on what "skill" I want to use, I feel as though I have to be in a different frame of mind for each, as if I am using a totally different part of my mind. I know I am not alone in these experiences. Many of you can relate, as can I, to the ability to know and remember certain facts and skills regarding our jobs, but we cannot remember the name of a person we met just five minutes ago. We might be able to do complex tasks that most people are not capable of doing, yet we have trouble remembering what we had for lunch yesterday. So in one case, we feel super smart, but then in another case we feel like a total idiot.

The same goes for the art of "thinking" vs. the art of "sensing." When I am thinking or remembering something, I feel I am using my brain in a more precise direct way. But when I am sensing things, such as in an empathic or psychic way, I feel I am using my brain in an entirely different way. "Thinking" is more like accessing data, while "sensing" is more like relaxing, opening up, and listening. The two functions could not be more different.

I am left wondering how many different "functions" our mind is capable of, but we are not yet aware of, because we mostly think of our brain in terms of "thinking." I suspect a lot of that gray matter we do not use might be associated with other skills and functions that we have yet to discover.

Honestly, your guess is as good as mine. I am not trying to pretend I know all the answers. I am just opening up the possibilities for thought and discussion. With that said, I do have some suspicions of what humans might be capable of. I do believe humans have super

183

powers they have yet to discover, or at least fully understand and utilize.

The main principle I have decided to discuss for this chapter is the idea of "mind over matter," literally. What I mean is that I believe humans have the potential ability to use their mind in a way that can influence and manipulate energy, to then have an impact on matter.

Energy is everywhere, and surrounds everything. Energy particles, or whatever you want to call them, make up the mass and structure of the energy. I like to think of energy as air with little dust particles in it. Imagine if you could organize and manipulate those dust particles in such a way that they could organize and work together to move an object. What if your mind could send out brainwaves or frequencies in the form of energy that can impact the energy surrounding an object? You might be able to impact and manipulate the energy surrounding an object enough to move the object.

We have all heard about people who can supposedly bend spoons. Science cannot prove how this happens, or if it is just some kind of magic trick. But the concept is not unheard of. Is the person bending the spoon with some kind of thought waves, an energy stream, or perhaps they are able to create heat focused on a certain spot to affect an object? Any way you slice it, if the claims are true, humans are able to affect objects not connected to them.

I believe in the future humans will be discovering and developing their unused brain power. What was once impossible or "magic," will be viewed as an explainable human skill that many are able to develop. Much like psychic ability, advanced and evolved skills that humans develop will no longer be stigmatized as weird or wrong in some way. People are always so scared of things they don't understand. Since the beginning of time, humans capable of incredible skills have been sometimes accused of working with the Devil or some trickery. That type of thinking is only a response out of fear and ignorance.

As humans further evolve and develop incredible abilities, we as a society will have to let go many of our "fear responses" to what we thought were odd or incredible skills. Instead of being confused and scared, resulting in condemning and banishing a person with odd abilities, we will have to embrace the person and ask how they did it.

I believe a major reason humans have not developed these new abilities, is because psychologically the person knows they will face horrible societal consequences as their "reward." Why in the world would anyone want to learn how to bend a spoon with their mind if it will result in being ostracized from society? Humans are basically "dumbed down" because of societal influence out of fear and ignorance.

An evolved human will have to overcome the fears of evolving so that they can evolve. Other humans and society will have to evolve so that they can accept humans evolving and developing skills they don't fully understand or can't yet do themselves. I won't hold my breath, but I know eventually the day will come.

A human having the ability to use their mind to manipulate energy around them is not the only super power I see. We also have two skills called "Astral travel" and "Remote viewing." They are both similar concepts and skills, but slightly differ.

Astral travel is defined as having an intentional "Out-of-Body Experience," such that your "astral body" (consciousness) can travel to destinations far and wide without you (your body) physically going there. I know this might sound a bit confusing and far-fetched. I am including it because it is not as far-fetched or ridiculous as it might sound once you look at the proposed mechanics.

If you believe everything is energy, and you believe your soul and consciousness are energy, then you would naturally believe that energy has the power of movement and travel just like energy waves, electrical impulses, and energy frequencies would be able to travel. If so, then it is conceivable that a human could develop a way to control this inner energy and release it for limited travel.

There are plenty of people, such as many who are psychic, that claim to have this ability to Astral Travel. There are old rumors and stories of how the military had programs to develop and use this concept. It is not that crazy, really, and some of us have experienced it in some limited or amazing ways.

Remote viewing, on the other hand, involves the same concept of viewing things from a distance, but the person's energy and consciousness remains in their body. Instead, the Remote Viewing would be more of a psychic process where they align with, or attach to, a frequency and "read" the information they receive. Remote viewing is much like a psychic communicating with the dead in the sense that they are opening their minds and trying to "sense" the energy. This is in contrast to Astral Travel, which you would actually be touching the energy with your own energy.

These concepts are also not as ridiculous as they sound. Plenty of people and psychics already claim to be doing this. These skills are not much different than meditation. Meditation is something we all can understand and relate to even if we have not participated.

Meditation is the art and skill of getting your mind into such a relaxed state, that you can take yourself places in your mind, or listen for, or sense, certain things or pieces of information a person might be seeking. Meditation is the beginning phase of many of the super powers to come. Meditation is the human's way of gradually dipping their toe into the water of evolved super powers.

For any of you who wish to experiment a bit with these concepts and dip your toe into the water, I recommend developing your meditation skills. With that said, I must confess, and I am embarrassed to say, I personally do not meditate. That is not my mode of operation. But I'm weird, so don't mind me.

If you are like me and meditation is not your thing, I recommend building your empathy and listening skills. Although I have not, and do not, meditate, I have done a lifetime of people-watching. I have developed very strong empathic and listening skills. This is my mode of operation. By using empathy, I am able to BECOME whatever or whoever I choose to focus on. So, in regards to the super powers mentioned above, my method for remote viewing would be to actually place my mind in the location I want to view. I would become a part of that location to such a degree that I can feel everything there. It is an art of putting yourself in perfect alignment with what you want to sense and then BECOMING what you are trying to sense. It is difficult to explain to those who have never done it.

The important thing is that there are multiple methods to reach the same destination. Others, such as psychics, will have different opinions and methods from what I have explained and discussed. They will also say I have over-simplified the concept, which I have. I am not trying to claim I have the right way, or only way for anything. Also, I would have to write an entirely separate book to fully explain all the various psychic concepts and abilities. My purpose here was only to introduce the premise and concept that humans have the potential to develop very highly advanced skills and abilities if we continue to evolve.

CHAPTER TWENTY-THREE

Colonization

Colonization? Colonization of what? What am going to ramble on about now? Well, I am not talking about a colon, which is part of your digestive system. Nor am I talking about colonialism that went on in our world history with the major world powers who took over occupied land for their own purposes. I am referring to colonization on a more evolved grand scale, such as on Mars or other unsettled areas.

We are running out of places to live. Land and natural resources are growing more scarce. Population keeps increasing. Pollution and deforestation are increasing. The mathematics of the situation is not in our favor. It seems at some point humans will need to colonize underutilized or new areas, for human habitation, natural resource mining, or use of some kind.

Where will that be? That is the question. Let us preface our discussion by setting aside all political arguments. This is not a chapter on climate change, global warming, or any other scientific/political argument. However, let it be noted that the term "scientific/political" should not even be a thing. It's a paradox. That aside, let us stand together on the commonality that we all acknowledge the Earth is deteriorating in the form of increased pollution, the oceans filling with garbage, air quality declining, and water access and quality declining. The population increases while the available land remains the same, or is even decreasing due to flood, drought, and fire, among other things. Can we all agree on that mostly? The reasons don't matter for right now. Let's not even discuss those. We are having a lovely holiday meal all together and there will be no screaming at the table.

So, we have a problem. We will need to find new horizons and expand for reasons of habitation, natural resources, and perhaps even survival if things come to that. Where shall we go? The moon? Mars? The ocean? Antarctica? Space stations? Northern Canada? (I just felt the entire country of Canada cringe). We have to go someplace, so where will it be?

People have romantic visions of humans building some grand base on Mars. I really do not know why this is. I truly don't. You cannot even walk outside without a space suit, not to mention that the gravity is not correct there. We would have to build huge domes and shelters, which we would not be able to leave. How would we get all the building materials there in our lifetimes? Are people really going to want to travel to Mars so they can live as a prisoner in a manufactured dwelling they can never leave? Maybe you would. I am just asking. Regardless of your answer, I am not seeing the romance in the idea.

Would it be easier to build the same kind of manufactured dwellings and communities under the ocean? They would have to be water proof just like those on Mars would have to be air tight. You would be stuck and not able to leave living under the ocean, just like living on Mars. You could stare out the windows at fish all day, but you would need powerful lights, because it's actually very dark under the ocean. Are you okay not seeing the sun anymore? Maybe you should try a winter in Norway before answering that question with confidence. I mentioned Norway because it sounds like a wonderful country to me, but I wondered how I would do during the winter there. As it is, I get depressed after two days of clouds. So how do you think I would do in Norway, or under the ocean? I live in southern California for a reason folks.

So far, I do not feel we are doing well. Shall we try Antarctica? I don't think it is deathly cold year-round. I hear summers can be nice, and there is actually a tourist industry there. Sort of. For ships anyway. We have communities and research bases on Antarctica already. Notice I said "on" Antarctica. It's as if I am trying to decide in my mind if I would be "in" a "place" on an actual land mass, or ON a thick sheet of ice that could eventually break off and float away, or worse, melt. Who knows. I know the scientists know, and we are learning more about Antarctica all the time. Who knows the amazing treasures and prehistoric civilizations that might lie beneath all the white snow and ice that we can see?

If we did develop Antarctica, we would have to know what exactly we are building on, if it would remain stable, and our structures would have to sustain the inhumane cold winters. You would once again be stuck inside and not able to leave. And no, I am not talking about "Minnesota winter" stuck inside. I mean, seriously cannot leave or you die winter conditions. Those folks in Minnesota can still go out during winter, and many of them would even jump into a frozen lake if you dared them to. I used to live in New England and I would go outside in the winter with a t-shirt on, so I totally get it. But there would not be any of that living on Antarctica. However, it is an option I suppose.

What else we got? Northern Canada and the North Pole region? Honestly, I am not sure Canada wants all of us up there. I am not going to even consider that as an option without prior approval from all my Canadian neighbors and friends. I have too much respect for that beautiful country, much of which is still untapped and not riddled with pollution and waste.

Don't even get me started on the moon. Rumor has it, the dark side of the moon is already taken by aliens. I say that tongue and cheek, but do I? Regardless, the moon is not much better than Mars other than the fact it is closer. And space stations? Well, I am actually going to have a little discussion about space stations in the next chapter, so I will shuffle that discussion over there.

I don't know about you, but I feel like we are hitting a wall. All of our potential sites would require incredible expense, technology, and we would end up very limited in our quality of life, as well as our ability to have freedom of movement. You know what? I am starting to wonder if maybe it might be easier to somehow repair and improve what we already have. The land we have currently settled here on Earth is really nice. We are free to roam about, travel, and much of the area does not require advanced super-tech shelters for survival. Well, except Minnesota in the winter. But they manage just fine.

Imagine all the money required to build colonies on Mars. Trillions in any currency. It is not much different for developing the ocean floor. Further developing Antarctica is not actually cheap either. What could we do if we took all the money on "colonization," and instead invested it all in repairing, renewing, and redeveloping our existing "colonies" here on Earth? Could we clean up and curb the pollution, water, and air issues? Do I hear a scientific "yes" on that?

I am not suggesting any kind of political agenda. It is fine if you disagree and would rather live on Mars. I have nothing against that. I am just exploring our options through a common-sense lens of commonality for a problem we all have whether we care to admit it or not. Considering all our options, the expense and limitations, I vote we focus on Space Ship Earth.

No, the chapter does not end here. Sorry, I know some of you might have been hoping for that at this point. There is a larger point to be made here. We were faced with a problem. We have a huge mess right here in our own backyard. We explored leaving and going elsewhere to solve it. It really wasn't feasible. It actually makes more sense to spend and invest in our current backyard. It makes more sense to solve the problems we have here, rather than making bigger more expensive and limiting problems by moving elsewhere.

This is an analogy for life. Sometimes our life is such a mess, that it seems it might be inevitable that we have to "leave" and go elsewhere. This can apply to our personal relationships, job, housing, family, community, or a variety of things. There might be so much "pollution" and "damage" that it seems too much of a mess, and even hopeless. We consider just giving up and starting over elsewhere with different people.

Sometimes leaving and starting over is the correct decision. It depends on the circumstances. But more often than not, it makes more sense and is "cheaper" to focus on what you have, where you are, and instead work on solutions to solve your problems and improve your situation.

An evolved person examines a situation and problem in a very pragmatic, logical, and organized way. You can apply all the tools we have covered in this book. You can carefully analyze the problem, and consider various solutions. Also consider all of the consequences resulting from each solution. Once you have a clear and logical understanding of the situation, you can make a logical and strong decision about what to do. You can make the correct choice without fear. Fear will prevent you from making the correct choice. Set fear aside and make a good choice based upon correct thinking, facts, logic,

192

and what is most closely in alignment with your beliefs and desires.

All of this is easier said than done. Life is not easy, and is usually complicated. However, an evolved person is no longer afraid to THINK, CHANGE, and ACT. As a human, you will still make mistakes. You will still make the wrong choice sometimes. That is okay. If you end being wrong, that does not mean you failed. Going through this process and getting it wrong is better than sitting in a lump and doing nothing.

If you consistently follow your new process of working through your feelings, problems, and desires, you will eventually end up in a much better position than if you did not. The best way to solve problems is usually to start at home, within yourself, in your mind. In the next chapter we will discuss more about this, and the need to do your "shadow work" in the dark depths of space. Until then, remember to believe in yourself for who you are and what you can become if you so choose. You do not need to go elsewhere. Focus on yourself and your present home that is within your heart and soul. Looking inward within your own backyard first is proof you are evolving.

CHAPTER TWENTY-FOUR

Space Exploration

What in the world is a chapter on space exploration doing in a book like this? Well, this is a book on evolving, and I think space exploration will be a part of our evolution. But more importantly, I feel examining our inner yearning for space exploration helps us realize more about ourselves while we are here on Earth.

Yes, I realize we are already exploring space. Sometimes I do not watch the news much and I spend periods of time living under a rock, but I fully realize we have already done our fair share of space exploration. However, I am not talking about launching satellites to roam the Universe, or taking trips to the moon or the International Space Station. I am talking about the potential idea of a large crew of humans exploring the galaxy in a starship. Yes, I know I have watched too many episodes of *Star Trek*, and those of you who read my book *The Walk-In* know I was in one of the movies, for which I have to mention when I write a book because I am such a fan-girl of the entire *Star Trek* franchise. But my own Sci-fi *Star Trek* fetishes aside, I think it is very likely we eventually reach a level of technologically where we are able to do some deep-space travel.

Our first substantial space travel with large amounts of people may very well be to Mars. But I believe eventually we will construct a large space station with propulsion to travel. I believe I just described a starship. How far, how fast, and how many people can be carried, all depends on the level of technology we are able to develop. I do not believe we currently have the technology necessary. Our current understanding of physics, time, propulsion, and travel are too inferior to accommodate substantial true deep-space travel that is practical and useful.

Any technology that requires "burning fuel" is simply not going to work. Storing enough fuel for such a mission, along with the rate of speed traditional fuel can propel us, is just not workable. I believe the breakthrough is going to come in a way that is outside our current "box" of thinking. I feel the breakthrough might come with our study of wormholes and how the traditional "A to B" travel can be violated and subverted by using mechanisms that the Universe naturally provides us if we can gain a full understanding of them. I also believe there will be a way to propel and travel a starship at the speed of light. Honestly, we actually need something faster than that. But my little mind can at least imagine our science being able to figure out speed of light travel for a vessel.

Clearly, we have a lot of work to do if we are to reach this level of travel. If all of this talk is a bit too unrealistic for your mind, then let us for a moment stick to the idea of a large group of humans traveling to Mars. That seems realistic for most people. So, why would anyone want to do this? Why would anyone want to get on a spaceship for a long journey through space to Mars or anywhere else out there?

I guess the question would be why people do anything? Curiosity? Adventure? Because they are bored on the couch? Would YOU want to travel through space to some far-off destination? Why? Human psychology will usually give you one of two answers. The first answer is to go toward something out of curiosity. The second answer is to get away from something they do not like. So, are you the type of person that will go toward anything just for the experience and curiosity? Or are you a person who desires to get away from something, and where you are going is not that important as long as it gets you away from something?

In other words, would you travel in space because you are curious about what else might be out there, or would you space travel because you want to leave Earth? The answer is important, although both answers reveal flaws within us. If you would space travel because you are curious and want to see what is there, then that raises the question of why explorations of Earth and your own inner being are not enough to make you curious. If your space travel desires are in response to just wanting to get away from Earth, then a person has to wonder why you think leaving Earth is going to solve whatever issues and complaints you are trying to leave behind.

Humans tend to have deep inner "demons" or issues that we cannot easily understand or solve. A human's common response to this is to seek an escape so they no longer need to spend the energy facing their inner issues. Humans can go toward something else, or leave something behind. Either way, a human's instinctual response is to TRAVEL, or alter their current location. Why? Well, for some reason humans associate their inner issues with where they are at that moment. It is as if the issues and problems are screwed down into the ground at that location, but they themselves can leave. In this way, people think they can escape their problems by leaving.

This chapter is toward the end of the book for a reason. Yes, space travel is a more "evolved" concept, so it makes sense it comes later in the book, BUT the better reason is because we have spent this entire book taking a journey to leave the old, and travel to the new. While this was necessary and helpful, there also comes a time when we must do some "shadow work" and examine WHY we feel we had to do what we did. Why did we so badly want to take a journey away from the old and into the new?

I believe it was because we were in pain at some level, struggling at some level, or just generally uncomfortable in some way. So why not leave that and travel away from it, and reach perhaps a better destination? It all sounds good, and it's helpful to a degree, and for a time. But I hope you have realized by now that there is a lot of heavy lifting required in our self-work as humans trying to "fix" ourselves, and then evolve. We have to face fears, problems, and issues within ourselves. We have been doing much of that work.

It does not matter if we travel hundreds of miles down the road, long distances across the seas, or epic distances by air. It does not matter if we jump into a starship and travel to a different planet or across the galaxy. At some point, a person has to take the time to examine what is inside us. Ironically, a person does not need to travel a single yard or meter to do the toughest self-work. To a degree, traveling across the galaxy might be easier than taking a journey through our deepest and darkest most inner thoughts, fears, and issues.

Let me ask you something else. If you were somehow able to solve all your inner issues and felt a complete sense of well-being, inspiration, excitement, and fulfillment, would you even want to travel through space? If you were happy and loving life, why would you want to risk your life, stuffing yourself into a cramped limited spaceship that was heading to places where there was no atmosphere or environment to even support life? That would be one of those "What am I doing and why am I doing it?" moments for sure.

Traveling into space is like being a goldfish that desires to live outside of water. Why would a goldfish want to do that? A goldfish needs to be in water that is oxygenated and within a certain temperature range. If you take the goldfish out of that, they would have to exist in some sort of little baggie of water that can sustain a certain temperature and somehow gets oxygen. The goldfish would be trading in a large fishbowl for a tiny baggie of uncomfortable water. Why? Because they want to see what it's like? Or because they wanted to leave the fishbowl for some reason? It is not long before logic sets in and these questions arise, and one would question the sanity of the motivations.

Please do not misunderstand me, I am not trying to discourage space travel. I think we will eventually explore space on a grand scale for scientific and curiosity reasons. But since this book is about evolving ourselves, it is more important for me to point out the psychological perspectives.

I predict for many people, they would end up feeling like Dorothy from *Wizard of Oz*. They would eventually realize that "there is no place like home." The goldfish would realize that its large fishbowl with oxygen and correct water temperature was not such a bad deal. If the goldfish was unhappy, maybe it's easier to focus on exactly why it was unhappy, and work on solutions, rather than just wanting to leave.

I believe humans would come to realize that being limited to a starship or being stuck in a space suit would become tiresome. They would miss being free, outside in the air under the EARTH sky, smelling the air, listening to the birds, and being fully present in their native and correct natural environment of Earth. And if there were reasons they wanted to leave Earth, maybe it might be easier to focus on those problems and come up with solutions, rather than leaving for a more limited existence just to get away.

We call this "shadow work" because we must go into the dark recesses of our mind and face issues we have always wanted to avoid. These issues float around in the dark depths of space within

198

our own mind and soul. This is the most difficult space travel you will face. But traveling into the darkness of space within your own mind to examine and face your most inner issues can result in incredible breakthroughs and freedom for yourself.

Eventually, humans will have the opportunity to travel in space and do deep-space exploration. But first, they will have to do substantial deep-space exploration within their own minds and souls. They will have to find the answers they are seeking, within themselves first, before seeking them out in the Universe. Humans will first have to evolve.

CHAPTER TWENTY-FIVE

What Is The
Meaning Of Life?

O ther than "What came first, the chicken or the egg?" the question of "What is the meaning of life?" is one of the most pondered questions among humans on Earth. I will attempt to answer both of these questions.

Let's get the easy one out of the way first. What came first, the chicken or the egg? Clearly, if you are to believe in a more "Big Bang" scientific approach, the egg came first. The only way a chicken could have come first is if "someone" or "something" put a chicken here. Otherwise, like most life, there would have been some accidental natural occurrence that led to the creation of eggs that hatched chickens.

As I describe in my book *The Hunter Equation*, I believe our world was a result of a Singularity, where there was a massive explosion (Big Bang) from a Black Hole. Earth would have been created by accident, with debris gathering together. The key phrase is "by accident." I believe life on our planet likely started the same way, meaning, by accident. Thus, an egg would come first, then a chicken after.

But what about humans? Humans don't come from an egg, so humans cannot have existed "by accident." True. Very true. This is why I believe humans were put here by some external force, meaning, by some other beings or civilization, as *Homo sapiens* who then evolved into today's human race.

This would beg the question then, if humans were "put here," then how come chickens could not have been "put here?" Well, they could have been. In that case, chickens came first, then eggs. So I guess the question remains. As it should. But I have my opinion and you have yours.

What about God? Didn't God create our world? Yes, I believe God did create our world. Except didn't I just say that our world was created from a Black Hole? Now I am saying God created it? Which is it? Oh, come on folks, we are all more evolved now, right? I thought we discarded that binary thinking.

BOTH of my statements can be true at the same time. How? Well, if God created the massive Black Hole explosion that created our world, then God did indeed create our world and everything in it. Add to that the fact that I believe God and the Universe are the same thing. It is as if my theories are consistent with both scientific beliefs AND some religious beliefs. The binary thinkers like to believe it is one or the other, and argue with each other. However, the truth is usually in the middle, and both science and God could exist together at the same time, depending on your definition of "God."

I promised myself that I would not bring politics or religion into this book. Now look what I have done. Do I delete what I have just written, or can I trust all of us to be reasonable enough to accept different conjectures even if you personally believe something different? I think we are all evolved enough to listen and decide what to leave behind and what to bring with us. I am also trying to illustrate that none of us know exactly the true nature of the situation. More importantly, I am trying to show that different conflicting beliefs might actually share some of the same truth. Remember commonality? Even if we disagree, we can find some areas of commonality and agreement. That is what evolved people do.

Okay, one last major question before we dive into the main event. For extra bonus points, "Why did the chicken cross the road?" Anyone? Well, after many years contemplating this question, especially when I was bored in math class during my school years, I have concluded that the chicken crossed the road simply to get to the other side. The much larger more important question would be, "Why did the chicken WANT to cross the road?" And this folks, leads us into our original major question.

What is the meaning of life? I spent most of my life not knowing the answer to this question. It was not until I began my spiritual journey by fire, that I received my first satisfying answer. I asked my (seemingly mostly alien) mentor this question. Without hesitation his answer to me was, "To make a difference." That was his answer to what the meaning of life is. I don't know whether it was because I believed everything he said, or because he was a certified genius, or because it was a correct answer, but that reply really resonated and rang true for me. That answer became my foundational basis for many of my beliefs going forward.

However, with all that said, I have evolved, grown, and expanded my own thinking over the years to believe the answer to that question is much broader than just those few words of "to make a difference."

I have developed my own belief that the eternal human soul is seeking to ever-expand and grow, so as to mirror the actual Universe itself. I believe the Universe is a sphere that is ever-expanding outward, as everything that exists is inside the sphere. The term infinity is real and exists because, and only because, the Universe is always expanding, thus there is never an end. Also, because the Universe is always expanding outward and growing, it cannot be defined. Even if you could define its location and border, it would be totally different one second later since it would have expanded and grown during that one second.

Therefore, I also agree that God is without limits, since God is aligned with the Universe. I am not trying to bring religion back into the discussion. I am just trying to show that the different theories and beliefs actually align with each other more than people care to admit. A person does not need to believe in one belief, or another belief, or even both beliefs. A person can believe in no belief. But our commonality is that we are all still here, together, wondering what the answer is to the question.

I believe our eternal souls, consisting of cosmic and divine energy, are always with God if you believe that, or are part of the Universe if you believe in that, and our souls are seeking to expand and grow infinitely just like the Universe. What is the best way for something intelligent to grow and evolve? Through experiences would be the best answer I would think. Thus, our souls are seeking new experiences so that they can evolve and grow. To me, that is the meaning of life. To grow and evolve. The title of this book was not a complete accident. I believe the title of the book is the meaning of life.

With all this in mind, what might you say to yourself or someone who asks, what you are doing here? What is your purpose? Based on this discussion so far, you might reply to them, "I am here to have experiences, learn, grow, and evolve." That right there would be a fantastic answer.

This should raise all kinds of questions within yourself about whether or not you are living up to your purpose and meaning. Are you living your life to have experiences, learn, and grow? Or are you living for some other purpose? Are you living in order to get more money to buy a bigger house? Is that your meaning of life? Or are you living to watch TV all day? Or maybe you are not living at all? Maybe you are living in fear of having experiences, and therefore not having experiences. Maybe you avoid having experiences, learning, or doing anything outside your comfort zone. Why are you doing that? Do you have some issues you need to work on and clear out of your mind, body, and soul? Maybe you will consider making some changes? It is not for me to judge or decide. I am only raising thoughts to be contemplated.

If the meaning of life is to grow and evolve, then you are not truly living life to the fullest unless you are growing and evolving. I'll leave that thought sitting there to be contemplated by you.

Based upon this line of thinking and logic, a person would be eager to seek out new experiences that will give them new knowledge, perspectives, and meaning to their existence. Do not be afraid to have these experiences. Invite and embrace them. However, I do not believe experiences alone are the only thing we are seeking.

I believe Love is the language of God and the Universe. Love is a major foundation of all existence. If there is such a thing as "the light" and "the dark," love would be the basis for "the light," while fear would be the basis for "the dark." It is no accident that I have stressed the importance of getting rid of fear. When you get rid of fear, you get rid of darkness. Conversely, when you embrace love, you BECOME "the light." You will recall that being in full alignment with, and BECOMING what you wish to feel and sense, is the key to advanced abilities and thinking.

The Universe, space, is a dark place. It is literally dark, as in, "can't see much." People are normally scared of the dark. The dark feeds our fears of the unknown, and the unknown scares us. However, our souls are made of energy, and energy is light. The light of our soul can exist in the darkness of space with the knowledge that we ARE the light. We then give light to the darkness, which is then not as scary.

Not to get too far from my point, we will bring things back around and remind ourselves that our light burns eternally on love, which gives us hope. If we have love, we have hope. If we have hope, we still have love somewhere within us. If we are temporarily missing both, we reach out toward others who will show compassion and love, and reignite our light with love and hope.

Love is such an important basis of our existence that I believe our soul is constantly seeking to experience love in many different ways. Our soul is always trying to be wrapped in love, immersed in love, and wants to be a part of love. What better way to do this than to seek any and all ways to experience love.

I believe this is why many people will chase one relationship to the next, even if it seems illogical at times. Humans are always trying to gain new perspectives and insights into love. Our experiences with different people, different activities, states of being, and so forth, give us different experiences with love.

We all can relate to the fact that we feel different kinds of love for different people and things. Our love for mother/father, brother/sister, romantic partners, pets, friends, places, activities, hobbies, and so forth, all bring with them a different type of love. Our soul knows this and is always seeking new and different perspectives on love. Thus, a person could say that the meaning of life is to experience love in as many different ways as possible.

So back to the very important question. Why did the chicken WANT to cross the road? That is up to the chicken. The chicken was seeking something. Does it really matter what the chicken was seeking? I argue it does not. The chicken gets to decide what it is seeking, and for its own reasons. However privileged this chicken seems, I believe you have the same privileges. YOU get to decide what

205

you are seeking.

The meaning of life is for each human to discover their own meaning. So now what would you tell someone if they asked you what the meaning of life is, or what your purpose is? It is not for me to answer that for you. I believe you can come up with your own great answer that has meaning for you. The only thing that must remain constant is that you feel your life has meaning, and that you are seeking that meaning. Go and do what will answer those questions for you. Spend your time with those that help you on your journey to answer those questions. That is your journey now. Your journey is to seek and live the meaning of life.

CHAPTER TWENTY-SIX
Fly Away

Our journey is coming to an end. But your journey is just beginning. This book was not just about evolving. I hope you are beginning to see by now that this book was about healing. This book was about giving yourself second, third, fourth, fifth, and infinite chances to become better, and to live again. This book is about rebirth and renewal.

I started this book with the premise that you might be in pain or struggling with something in your life. Or, perhaps you just wanted to learn more and improve your already great life. For whatever reason, this book found you, or you found this book. I found you or you found me. I am grateful you decided to take this journey with me, and you packed what served you, and you left the rest behind. We then hit the road, and off we went on a grand adventure.

I have desperately tried to not tell you what to think or who you should be. I tried to show you new ways of HOW to think, so that you can think whatever you want. I have tried to show that you can do or become anything you want. Anything is possible. I want you to be what YOU want to be.

I hope you learned a lot. But mostly, I hope you learned more about who you are and who you want to become. I hope you learned that you can be a unique individual of your own choosing. I hope you learned that you can find new hope and new possibilities. You can find happiness again if you had lost it. You can live again if you thought you had died inside. You can live better if you thought before you couldn't.

But even more than those things above, I wanted to inspire you to BELIEVE again. I want you to believe in magic. Magic is your ability to evolve and change your own life. I want you to believe you can step outside your present life and construct a life that better serves you. Believe in magic. Believe in yourself. You are the magic.

Realize how valuable and amazing you are. Realize how amazing you can become. It does not matter your current circumstances in life. You are deeply valued. Do not believe the people who make you feel less than who you are. Do not believe the negative voices in your head telling you the same. Instead, remember our journey and the possibilities you have seen. Remember how I reminded you of your incredible value and worth as a human, and eternal soul of light within the Universe. Your value is infinite and priceless. Do not let anyone convince you otherwise.

I know despite all you have learned, there are some of you who still might feel lost or sad for some reason. Some of you will revisit certain chapters of this book. Some of you will need to digest and contemplate what we have discussed. But please know that my goal was not just to help you evolve. My primary goal was to help you heal from whatever needed healing. Or more specifically, I my goal was to help you learn to heal yourself.

Please do not let other people, events, or life, defeat you. Don't give up. I believe in you. Please believe in yourself. Give yourself a chance to survive, grow, and thrive. I have tried to provide you with a journey that would spark your imagination, your mind, and your spirit. It is up to you to take what serves you, and leave the rest behind.

Don't you see? How we began is now how we are ending. It is time for you start a new phase and journey of your life with what you have learned. It is time for you to jump on the road, sail on the high seas, and fly free in the sky like an eagle. It is time for you to fly away.

Where will you go? What will you do? It's up to you. Evolving is not the destination. Evolving is the mode of transportation to help you reach any destination you choose. Hopefully you have some skills now that you did not have before, or perhaps did not use before.

If evolving is your mode of transportation, healing is your motivation for the journey. Deciding to heal from your most inner wounds allows you to live fully. It allows you to have the courage for change. It allows you to dare to dream again. Your wounds can make you weak when they are first sustained, but once they are healed, you are far stronger than you ever were before. Healing is wisdom. Healing is strength. Healing is freedom.

A bird with a broken wing cannot fly. But once healed, the bird is free to fly away. Healing is freedom. You are not trapped or stuck. You can choose to heal, and to change. Change is our most important tool. Do not be afraid to use it. Use change like the wind that can lift your wings up into the sky of freedom, just as it powered your sails on the sea, and it provided inspiration as it blew on your face in the car.

If you ever feel that you have run out of fuel, please remember that Love is a fuel that never runs out or dies. Your love for things in life, your love for your enduring strength and hope, and your love for the things most dear to you in the Universe, is a love that can fuel you eternally. Your love toward others, both here and those who passed, will fill your own heart with love and fuel for life.

Hope in itself is love. Never lose hope. Remember, things always change. When life gets difficult, remember that things will change. Use your tools for causing change to happen more quickly. Just as with love, give hope freely to others. Love, and live by love. Live with hope, and give hope when it is needed.

I tried my best to inspire you with love and hope in this book. But it is up to you to continue the chain. Try to inspire others when you are able. Giving the gift of hope and inspiration is perhaps the greatest expression of love there is. Sometimes what we need most is some hope and inspiration.

I am honored to have taken this journey with you. I might not know your name, but I know your spirit. Anyone who is wanting and willing to take such a journey is definitely someone who has a spirit I admire and respect. I will remain with you in spirit, and you have my most sincere wishes for healing, happiness, and success. Use what you have learned, become what you wish to be, and live as an example to others of what humans can evolve into. Much love to you. Now fly away and be free.

ACKNOWLEDGEMENTS

Thank you Sarah Delamere Hurding for your editorial assistance, encouragement, and endless support.

Thanks to all of my clients and benefactors who have supported my mission of helping people become greater, stronger, more self-empowered, and free of pain.

Thank you to all the great musical artists whose music helped me create my own lyrics of magic within this book.

Also, by Brian Hunter

Heal Me is a powerful and touching book that will pull at your heartstrings, give you practical advice on overcoming a variety of life traumas, and will put you on the road to recovery and healing. *Heal Me* examines such issues as the death of a loved one, loss of a pet, suicide, anxiety, addiction, life failures, major life mistakes, broken relationships, abuse, sexual assault, self-esteem, living in a toxic world surrounded by toxic people, loneliness, and many other issues. This is a self-care book written in a very loving, practical, and informative way that you can gift to yourself, family, young people, and friends, as a gesture of love, support, and hope.

Rising To Greatness is a self-help book that takes you on a step-by-step transformation, from the ashes of being broken and lost, to the greatness of self-empowerment, accomplishment, and happiness. This book includes such topics as developing your sense of self, eliminating fear from your life, mastering your emotions, self-discipline and motivation, communication skills, and so much more.

The Hunter Equation is a practical spirituality book covering many topics, including life after death, reincarnation theory, cycle of life and death, human and animal souls, destiny vs. free will, synchronicities, Karma, soul mates, twin flames, angels, the future of humans, and many more topics. This is also the original book to unveil and fully explain the Hunter Equation life tool, and why it is far more relevant and accurate than The Law of Attraction.

Aliens: The Alien Agenda is a groundbreaking book that explores the existence of aliens in space, along with aliens already here on Earth. In addition to the author providing his own abduction and paranormal experiences, *Aliens* examines new plausible theories of why they are here, what they are hoping to gain, and how they are working to achieve it. *Aliens* also examines ideas surrounding spaceships, space travel, abductions, what the government knows, alien society, and the alien psychology. You will find in *Aliens* thoughts, ideas, and theories, that you have not seen elsewhere. This book truly brings with it a new perspective of how we think of aliens, and how aliens think of us.

The Walk-In is a memoir that takes you on a personal life-long journey, from childhood, through coming-of-age discoveries, successes, failures, and deep depressions, and struggles. The book describes paranormal events, resulting in the development of psychic abilities. This book is a very raw and honest adventure, with illicit scenes and subject matter, which is not for the faint of heart.

Made in the USA
Coppell, TX
20 September 2021

62717096R00118